Flies for Bass & Panfish

BY DICK STEWART & FARROW ALLEN

Book Design and Illustrations • Larry Largay
Photography • Dick Stewart
Cover Flies • Joe Messinger, Jr.

Published by Mountain Pond Publishing
P.O. Box 797
North Conway, NH 03860
USA

Distributed by Lyons & Burford
31 West 21 Street
New York, NY 10010
USA

Printed in the United States of America by Capital Offset Company

First edition. Second printing.

Library of Congress
        Stewart, Dick.
            Flies for bass & panfish / by Dick Stewart & Farrow Allen ;
        book design and illustrations, Larry Largay; photography, Dick
        Stewart — 1st ed. — Intervale, NH, USA : Northland Press ;
        New York, NY, USA : Distributed by Lyons & Burford, c1992.
            vii, 80, [7] p. : col. ill. ; 29 cm. — (Fishing flies of North America ; 3rd)
            Includes bibliographical references (p [83]) and index.
            ISBN 0-936644-10-9 (hardcover). — ISBN 0-936644-11-7 (softcover)

        1. Flies, Artificial—North America. 2. Bass fishing—North America. 3.
        Panfish fishing—North America. 4. Fly tying.   I. Allen, Farrow. II. Title.
        III. Title: Flies for bass and panfish. IV. Title: Bass & panfish. V. Series.
        SH451.S71725 1992   688.7'912—dc20   93-135248
                                            AACR 2 MARC

PREFACE

Because of its historical ties to British sporting tradition, fly fishing in the 1800s was associated with cold-water fisheries for trout and salmon, and flies tied specifically for bass and panfish were scarce, as were anglers who fished with them. In those times, if you didn't make your own flies you were hard pressed to find a source of supply. Often fly rodders discovered the fun of catching bass on flies quite by acccident. While casting for trout they found that their favorite stream or lake also contained bigger and brawnier black bass. During the late 1800s and early 1900s most bass flies were little more than oversize, broad-wing trout wet flies that were adapted for bass fishing.

Earliest bass "bugs" were fabricated with deer hair and yarn tied to a hook, and they were "dapped" or "jiggled" on a short line using a long cane pole. This technique was learned from local Indians and the lure was called a "bob" or "Jiggerbob." Although unlike modern fly fishing, this technique worked well and dapping is still popular for bass in many areas in the south, sometimes with flies but often with live minnows and frogs.

About 1912, outdoorsmen Emerson Hough and Fred Peet designed a fly with wings and body constructed entirely from natural bucktail. The fly had a gray or white body and a mixed wing of gray (or brown) and white hair. The fly was called the "Emerson Hough." Subsequent fly tiers began dressing it with deer-body hair instead of bucktail. The deer-body hair floated better and was often dyed in a variety of colors. The Emerson Hough and the Henshall Bug are good examples of early bass bugs.

Several tackle companies became actively involved in the early manufacture of flies and fly-rod lures for bass. One of the oldest was the Orvis Company of Manchester, Vermont. Orvis custom tied bass flies. The Henshall Bug, named for Dr. J.A. Henshall the author of the *Book of Black Bass* (1881), was marketed commercially by the Weber Life-like Fly Company. Others manufacturing bass flies in the early 1900s included the Creek Chub Bait Co., J. Hildebrandt, Co., James Heddon & Sons and E.H. Peckinpaugh who introduced the cork-body popper about 1910, and ultimately built a successful bass-fly company around it. Joe Messinger, Sr., developed the Bucktail Frog after World War I. This fly was so effective and realistic that it set the standard for deer-hair frogs to follow.

Following World War II, the rapid development of spinning tackle occupied the attention of bass fishermen and it wasn't until the late 1960s and 1970s that fly-fishing turned its attention again to fishing for bass. Meanwhile, Tom Nixon was learning to fish for bass and panfish in Missouri and Illinois. In the mid 1940s he moved to Louisiana and continued his lifelong devotion to his favorite quarry: bass and panfish. He created many unique fly patterns designed specifically for these warmwater fish. Nixon's freewheeling fly designs are both effective and interesting to tie. His 1968 book *Fly Tying and Fly Fishing for Bass and Panfish* documented fly designs up to that date and provided anglers with the first specific reference to a wide assortment of these flies.

During the 1970s the most profound changes took place in fly designs for bass and their warmwater relatives. Dave Whitlock, who had been designing trout flies for many years, turned his attention to flies for bass. Within a few short years Whitlock developed a wide assortment of ingenuous and attractive fly designs for bass. These were not ordinary flies. These were flies that embodied materials, techniques and colors that made them stand apart from all earlier flies. They looked alive! When Whitlock began gaining recognition for his bass patterns in the early 1970s, except for a few tiers like Tom Nixon, there had never been a tier of bass flies who was known nationally. Dave Whitlock opened a new chapter in the history of fly fishing and tying flies for bass, and he inspired many of the superb fly designs that were to soon follow. There is hardly a fly tier today who hasn't benefited from Whitlock's creative approach to designing flies that look as good to the angler as they do to bass. Not only do we have new fly patterns, Whitlock's use of nontraditional components inspired suppliers of fly-tying material to expand their selection to satisfy the newly emerged demand.

Concurrent with the development of new flies has been the modernization of the tackle used by fly fishermen. Foremost among these changes is the introduction of graphite fly rods, which has made casting large bass flies much easier. Improved fly lines, better hooks, the use of portable flotation devices such as float tubes - all are factors which have aided the development of warm-water angling.

Our emphasis in this book is on proven, successful fly designs for the beginner as well as the expert. Some flies are simple, other are complex, but all serve the angler well - they catch fish. We have not specified the sizes in which to tie these flies, nor do we suggest that the colors shown are the best ones to use. We consider size and color choices to be best determined by the fisherman based on many factors, such as the type of fish being sought, water clarity, realistic imitation, personal preference and availability of materials. We have avoided specific reference to brand names of hooks or materials because we believe that these matters, too, are best left to the discretion of the individual fly tier. You will also notice that we make no specific reference to the use of weed guards. While many flies are shown with weed guards of various types, we believe it is up to the tier to determine whether or not such a device is needed. Some waters are virtually weed free and a guard is unnecessary, in other locations a weed guard is indispensible. Which type of weed guard is best? We leave that up to you - look at the different styles and try them out for yourself.

We think it is safe to state that we have assembled here a collection of the best bass and panfish flies from some of the best fly tiers. We made a great effort to represent tiers from diverse parts of North America, and to include all of the notable bass fly tiers of whom we know. If we've omitted any important flies, or neglected any fly tier, the fault is entirely ours.

This book would not have been possible without extensive help and cooperation from others. Foremost among these are the many fly tiers who generously provided the flies to be photographed. It is said that a picture is worth a thousand words and our hope is that these photographs will provide a reliable reference for the fly-tying community. We owe a special thanks to Dave Whitlock, Tom Nixon, Larry Dahlberg, Tom Lentz and Jim Stewart for their extensive assistance. We are also very proud to have received the cooperation of notable fly-tiers such as Tim England, Jimmy Nix, Bob Clouser, John Betts, Joe Messinger, Jr., Billy Munn, Harry Murray, Eric Leiser, Lefty Kreh, Tom Farmer, Jack Ellis and Bob Popovics. To these tiers, and to all other contributors too numerous to mention, we wish to say thank you one and all.

Additionally we would like to thank Fran Stuart, Jack Russell and Bob Stewart for their editorial and technical assistance.

CONTENTS

Floating Bugs	2
Mice	10
Frogs	12
Crayfish	18
Leeches	20
Eels & Snakes	22
Divers	26
Jigs	29
Baitfish	30
Insects	60
Nymphs	66
Panfish Flies	72
Poppers	78

Tied by Tim England

'BECCA'S BUG

Hook: Straight eye, wide gape
Tail: Yellow and white fine rubber hackle over which is green medium rubber hackle
Skirt: Olive and yellow deer body hair over white
Legs: Yellow and white fine rubber hackle and green medium rubber hackle
Body: Rear half: Olive over yellow deer body hair stacked over white
Front half: Yellow, olive, black and white deer body hair spun and trimmed to shape

This tidy, little surface bug was tied by Tim England of Bellvue, Colorado, one of the recognized masters of clipped-deer-hair flies. He named this fly for his daughter, Rebecca. England uses a mixture of fine and medium rubber hackle to get more "bounce" in the legs, and the longer-than-normal rubber legs result in a fly that looks big, but casts like a small fly.

Tied by John Betts

BETTS' BULL-IT HEAD (FLASHDANCER)

Hook: Kinked shank popper hook
Weight: .025 lead wire, secured with Super Glue after the fly has been completed
Diving lip: Cut from sheet of .010 clear Mylar includes a long, narrow tapered stem that is folded in half, fitted under the "kinked" portion of the hook shank, pinched together and secured with thread wraps
Tail: Red marabou with copper crystal flash on the side
Body: A single strip of closed-cell foam, (Evasote) attached at the head behind the diving lip with equal lengths of foam extending from each side, almost like wings. The body is then formed in two steps, pulling first the left and then the right piece of foam back along the side of the hook, drawing them snug and tying them off at the rear
Eyes: Steel or brass plated black headed stainless steel dressmakers pins pushed through the length of the body, the excess clipped away

Tied by John Betts

BETTS' BULL-IT HEAD (FROG)

Hook: Kinked shank popper hook
Weight: Lead wire (See Bull-it Head - Flashdancer)
Diving lip: Clear Mylar (See Bull-it Head - Flashdancer)
Tail: Two very long grizzly saddle hackles tied flat and splayed out with olive marabou on top
Body: Closed-cell foam (See Bull-it Head - Flashdancer)
Eyes: Stainless steel pins (See Bull-it Head - Flashdancer)
Note: The final step for completing both Bull-it Heads is to color the body with waterproof marking pens as you see fit. This particular one has been marked with the colors of a frog.

John Betts of Denver, Colorado, is well known as an innovative fly tier who has pioneered in the use of synthetic materials and new fly styles. His original Bull-it Head, and one of the most popular, was tied all black and designed to look like a small bullhead minnow. Betts' Bull-it Heads perform like a Flatfish or Rapala minnow, and were likely the first of their kind to be offered commercially.

CRAZY-LEGS SPIDER

Hook: Straight eye, wide gape
Tail: Chartreuse rubber hackle
Legs: Chartreuse rubber hackle
Body: Chartreuse deer body hair, spun and clipped cylindrically, with a pointed nose
Eyes: Hollow plastic

Developed by Kevin McEnerney for fishing in lily pads where in clear, quiet water a lot of movement, rather than the noise of a popping bug, is wanted to get a bass' attention. Because of the large amount of rubber hackle used to construct the Crazy-Legs Spider, only a slight pull on the line is needed to set this bug dancing.

Tied by Kevin McEnerney

DAHLBERG DILG-SLIDER

Hook: Straight eye, wide gape, short shank
Tail: Red Flashabou over which is a chartreuse rabbit fur strip
Collar: Chartreuse deer body hair, clipped short
Sides: Grizzly hackle dyed chartreuse
Head: Chartreuse deer body hair, spun and trimmed into a rounded, blunt bullet head
Eyes: Hollow plastic
Note: For this fly to work properly the tail should be short and the head must be trimmed so that the shank of the hook is dead center in the cylinder-shaped head.

The early smallmouth bass slider known as the "Wilder-Dilg Slider" was originally constructed with a cork head, and dates back at least to the early 1930s. Heddon also marketed a "Wilder Dilg Feather Minnow" in a dozen colors. Dahlberg suggests fishing his Dilg-Slider with a ". . . rather steady retrieve, allowing it to make a gentle 'V' wake on the surface."

Tied by Larry Dahlberg

DAHLBERG HORSE POPPER

Hook: Straight eye, wide gape, heavy wire
Tail: A single pair of light olive grizzly neck hackles
Skirt: Light olive deer body hair
Head: Light olive deer body hair, spun and trimmed as shown and cemented on the bottom
Legs: Rubber hackle (optional)
Eyes: Hollow plastic eyes recessed into the deer hair head

Dahlberg's basic no-frills surface bug. About the Horse Popper, Dahlberg exclaims: "I flat-out guarantee this is the right shape and proportion to maximize the most important elements of a popping design . . . it will, day in and day out, produce more big bass than any other popper I've used."

Tied by Larry Dahlberg

Floating Bugs

Tied by Larry Dahlberg

DAHLBERG MEGA-SLOP SLIDER

Hook: Straight eye, stainless steel, heavy wire, 3X long and bent upward at a 30° angle
Tail: 20 to 30 mixed brown and black rubber hackles of varying lengths
Collar: Dyed brown deer body hair
Pectoral fins: (optional) Speckled hen body feather or similar on each side
Head: Brown and white deer body hair, spun and trimmed into a rounded, blunt bullet head
Eyes: Hollow plastic, yellow with black pupils
Whiskers: Dark moose mane or similar (optional)

A mega-version of the Dilg-Slider (which see) designed, in Larry Dahlberg's words "…to be fished in the heaviest cover…with a hook you could hang a cow on. The head will bounce off the cover and go around or over it rather than dig in like a popper or a diver." Color combinations range from black to white, and often the tail is composed of combinations of other materials such as feathers and crystal flash, but it's always kept short.

FLAT BUG

Hook: Straight eye, 4X to 6X long
Tail: Three pairs of furnace hackle, splayed outward
Skirt: Brown hackle, heavy
Legs: Three sets of brown rubber hackle, long
Body: Alternating bands of natural colored deer body hair, spun and trimmed very flat on the bottom and flat but slightly rounded on the top

Tied by Frank Theobald

Developed by Frank Theobald for largemouth and smallmouth bass fishing in Pennsylvania. The flat shape makes the Flat Bug fairly easy to cast yet offers a large silhouette when viewed from below. The long rubber hackles provide a lot of movement for fishing very slowly in clear, quiet water.

HENSHALL BUG

Hook: Standard dry fly
Tail: White bucktail
Body: Alternating bands of orange, red and white deer body hair, trimmed as shown
Wing: White bucktail tied spent and slightly back
Head: (optional) Spun natural white deer body hair, trimmed as shown

Tied by Dick Stewart

This is one of the oldest bass-fly patterns, named for Dr. James Henshall whose *Book of the Black Bass* was published in 1881. Henshall Bugs have caught countless bass and should not be ignored by the modern fly rodder. They are tied in a variety of styles and colors, including all white which serves as a simple, effective moth imitation.

JONATHAN

Hook: Straight eye, wide gape
Tail: Salmon pink rubber hackle
Skirt: Bright yellow hackle
Body: Yellow chenille
Legs: Salmon pink rubber hackle
Shellback: Dark red bucktail pulled forward
Head: The balance of the dark red bucktail is pulled forward and upward, cemented, squeezed flat, and trimmed as shown
Eyes: Hollow plastic, mounted high on the face of the head

This humorous and unusual looking bug was sent to us from Montreal by Canadian fly tier and bass fisherman Pierre Saumur, who uses this pattern when he wants to create a lot of noise and surface commotion. The Jonathan has accounted for many smallmouth bass in the St. Lawrence River.

Tied by Pierre Saumur

JUNE BUG

Hook: Straight eye, wide gape or popper hook
Tail: Black rabbit fur strip
Body: Balsa wood, shaped as shown with a flat nose at a 30° angle, lacquered black and painted
Eyes: Solid plastic, set high
Lip: A piece of clear, stiff flat Mylar sheet, trimmed and bent on each side as shown, cemented to the body and secured with fine brass nails and painted white in the center for better visibility

Tim England designed the June Bug after a well-known casting plug, the Arbogast Jitterbug. He describes it as being "kind of a top-water slider" that dances and gurgles around in the surface film. He also ties a version with a deer-hair body.

Tied by Tim England

PERKIOMEN MUDDLER

Hook: Down eye, 3X or 4X long
Tail: Light elk or deer body hair
Body: Pearl, silver or gold braided Mylar tubing, secured at the tail with red thread. Use a fairly large size of braided tubing, so the body will appear full
Wing: Light elk or deer body hair
Head and collar: Light elk or deer body hair, spun to form a collar and a clipped, cylindrical, squared-off head

This pattern was named after southeastern Pennsylvania's Perkiomen Creek by its developer Frank Theobald of Glenside, Pennsylvania. It is fished successfully either for largemouth or smallmouth bass, and has accounted for Theobold's largest catch in both species.

Tied by Frank Theobald

Floating Bugs

Tied by Dick Stewart

POWDER PUFF

Hook: Straight eye, wide gape
Body: Deer body hair - natural or dyed, in any combination of colors - spun and left untrimmed except for the removal of a small amount of hair around the bend of the hook to allow for more consistent hook-ups without actually exposing the hook point

This untrimmed gob of spun deer body hair was introduced to us by Tom Nixon who says it works best when the wind is blowing hard. It is carried by wind gusts and sent "…tumbling across the surface in a rather seductive fashion only to disappear in a maze of bubbles and spray." Another application for this mess of deer hair is its use in heavy cover. Fished over logs, deep into thick weeds or lily pads, it remains virtually weedless.

Tied by Claude Bedard

RICHELIEU

Hook: Straight eye, wide gape
Tail: Two pairs of ruffed grouse body feathers, curving out
Skirt: Natural deer body hair
Body: Natural, dyed brown, and black deer body hair, spun and clipped to a cigar shape as shown and cemented in front
Eyes: Hollow plastic, set into the body

The Richelieu was originated in the early 1980s by Claude Bedard of Cowensville, Quebec. It was named for the Richelieu River which drains Lake Champlain and enters the St. Lawrence River north of Montreal at Sorel. It has been a very successful bug for smallmouth fishing throughout the St. Lawrence and Richelieu Rivers, and most of the northern Lake Champlain watershed.

STEWART'S BUZZ BUG (PURPLE BACK)

Hook: Straight eye, wide gape, usually a large size
Spinner: 1" propeller between 6 mm plastic bead for a 1/0 hook - press down the barb to get the beads and propeller over the point
Tail: Paired white hackle outside of which are green and purple dyed grizzly hackles curving out; over this is bright green Flashabou over which is Gray Ghost crystal flash
Butt: Fluorescent orange chenille
Skirt: Green deer body hair on the sides, purple on the top
Body: Green and purple deer body hair, stacked over white deer body hair and trimmed flat on the bottom and rounded on the top as shown cemented in front and on the bottom
Eyes: Hollow plastic

Tied by Jim Stewart

Jim Stewart, a Florida architect, designed this fly to mimic popular wood or plastic surface bass plugs. When retrieved with short strips the propeller sprays water and causes a surface disturbance that attracts curious bass.

STEWART'S JOINTED POPPER

Extension tail: Blue, purple, white and black rubber hackle over which are pairs of light blue, teal blue and purple dyed grizzly (2 pairs) hackles curving out and copper crystal flash over all
Skirt: Light blue, teal blue and purple dyed grizzly hackles
Head: Fluorescent rose
Note: Cut the extension hook off at the bend and secure it to the front hook with a loop of stiff 20 lb. monofilament
Front section
Butt: Fluorescent rose chenille
Body: Purple, blue and black deer body hair stacked over black with an all white head, trimmed as shown, cemented front and bottom
Eyes: Solid plastic

The jointed tail of this popper never holds still. Even at rest the tail continues to swing from side to side. It's usually at this point when a bass hits it, says originator, Jim Stewart of Tampa, Florida.

Tied by Jim Stewart

STEWART'S SPIN-N-JIM

Extension Spinner: On a straight eye hook, mount 1" propeller between two 6mm rondelle clear plastic beads
Skirt: Black rubber hackle with a few strands of chartreuse and orange
Head: Black with a fluorescent orange stripe
Note: Cut the extension hook off at the bend and secure it to the front hook with a loop of stiff 20 lb. monofilament
Hook: Straight eye, wide gape
Butt: Fluorescent orange chenille
Body: Brown and tan spots of deer body hair stacked over black with a fluorescent orange head, trimmed as shown, cemented front and bottom
Eyes: Solid plastic, brown and black

Jim Stewart's Spin-N-Jim creates quite a commotion on the surface and draws aggressive bass from far away.

Tied by Jim Stewart

TAP'S DEER HAIR

Hook: Standard dry fly
Tail: Bright orange bucktail
Body: Orange, black and yellow deer body hair spun and trimmed as shown

This is a basic no-frills floating deer-hair bug that can be tied in any combination of colors. It was designed and promoted by Tap Tapply, a noted outdoor writer, and for many years bass fishermen considered this fly a reliable standard.

Tied by Tom Nixon

Tied by Umpqua Feather Merchants

WHITLOCK'S FLOATING MUDDLER

Hook: Down eye, 4X long
Underbody: Closed-cell foam
Body: Gold braided Mylar tubing, secured with red thread
Wing: Red, green and gold Flashabou, over which is yellow marabou topped with gold Flashabou and peacock herl
Collar: Black dyed deer body hair over light olive deer body hair
Head: Light olive deer body hair, spun and trimmed as shown
Eyes: Hollow plastic
Head: Red

Most Muddler Minnows tend to float because of their deer-hair head, in fact, trying to get them to sink is usually a challenge. Whitlock's floating version is tied with an oversize head and a foam underbody to insure that it keeps floating. It is often fished as if to struggle on the surface like a wounded minnow.

Tied by Umpqua Feather Merchants

WHITLOCK'S GERBUBBLE BUG

Hook: Straight eye, wide gape
Tail: A pair of orange hackles outside of which are brown grizzly hackles
Skirt: Dyed light brown grizzly and orange hackles, mixed - at this point you must tie on each side an orange and a brown grizzly hackle in front of the skirt. These will later be pulled forward along each side of the completed body to form the whiskerwings
Body: Dyed light brown deer body hair, spun and trimmed flat on top and bottom and cemented
Whiskerwings: Grasp hackles, fold the barbs to the outside and pull them forward and into the clipped deer hair body along a lateral line that parallels the hook shank and secure
Head: Bright orange deer body hair, spun and trimmed to follow along the lines of the body, and cemented

When it was introduced in the 1920s, the original Gerbubble Bug was laboriously constructed out of two pieces of balsa wood sandwiched together. This Dave Whitlock deer-hair version is simpler to tie and easier to cast.

WHITLOCK'S MOST WHIT HAIR BUG

Hook: Straight eye, wide gape
Tail: Fluorescent green marabou, chartreuse crystal flash and two strands of green rubber hackle outside of which is a bright green hackle and a shorter grizzly hackle
Skirt: Soft fluorescent green hackle and chartreuse crystal flash
Legs: Green, chartreuse and Speckled Flake chartreuse rubber hackle
Body: Spun chartreuse, black, red and orange deer body hair, clipped as shown and cemented in front and on the bottom
Eyes: Hollow plastic

This is Dave Whitlock's "basic" bass bug that he ties in many color variations. It is probably the quintessential bass fly and can be found in fly shops coast to coast.

Tied by Dave Whitlock

WIGGLE BUG (PURPLE)

Hook: Straight eye, long shank, wide gape, black finish
Tail: Purple marabou over which is pearl crystal flash
Body: Purple crystal chenille
Hackle: Black, palmered over the crystal chenille body
Diver head: A wedge shaped flat strip of purple closed-cell foam which is
        tapered toward the forward end. The foam is tied on top of the
        hook shank at the rear of the body, and the hook eye is inserted
        through the foam at the front
Eyes: Solid plastic

Designed by Larry Tullis for Edge Water Fishing Products of Clearfield, Utah, to imitate the swimming action of a Flatfish or Rapala type casting lure. The floating-diving foam head can be custom cut or purchased preformed or as part of a kit, and comes in a variety of colors.

Tied by Edge Water Fishing Products

WILKIE'S BEAUTY (YELLOW)

Hook: Straight eye, short shank, heavy wire
Wing: Gold Flashabou over which is yellow marabou interspersed with
        pearl crystal flash over which are strands of peacock herl and on
        each side a pair of webby grizzly hackles dyed yellow
Head: Spun yellow deer body hair with a center stripe of white deer
        hair, clipped flat on the bottom, rounded on the top and well
        cemented
Eyes: Hollow plastic

Al Wilkie, former President of the Federation of Fly Fishers, designed the "Beauties" for surface fishing on lakes and ponds in his native Texas. He suggests that other effective combinations include flies with a black head and orange wing; gray head and gray wing; purple head and white wing and an olive head with chartreuse wing.

Tied by Al Wilkie

YELLOW-CROWNED NIGHT HERON

Hook: Down eye
Tail: A segment of goose quill or other feather
Body: Pink crystal chenille
Throat: Pink crystal flash, tied long
Collar: Red deer body hair on the top and sides
Head: Yellow deer body hair and bright yellow deer body hair,
        trimmed flat and close to the hook on the bottom, flat but not
        as closely cropped on the top leaving most of the hair on the sides
        untrimmed

The Yellow-Crowned Night Heron was developed by Dana Griffin, III of Gainesville, Florida. It may be tied in a variety of colors except for the bright-yellow deer-hair head which is used with all flies. Although this bug may appear rough, Griffin insists that the "... hair must be trimmed flat on the bottom" and that "leaving long and stringy side hairs ... simulates the breathing and struggling behavior so attractive to gamefish."

Tied by Dana Griffin

Mice

Tied by Gary LaFontaine

CREATURE

Hook: Down eye, 3X or 4X long
Underbody: Closed cell foam, cut and slipped over the hook shank and secured with Super Glue and thread
Body: Gray chinchilla rabbit fur strip, wound over the underbody
Head: Gray rabbit fur

The Creature was designed by noted fly-fishing author and fly innovater Gary LaFontaine to represent a generic "small mammal." LaFontaine has observed that it is often more effective for bass than traditional deer-hair mice "because it rides very low in the water, pushing a sizeable wake."

Tied by Billy Munn

DEER-HAIR MOUSE

Hook: Straight eye, wide gape
Tail: Chamois or Ultra Suede
Body: Natural gray deer or caribou body hair, spun in alternating light and medium bands, and trimmed into the shape of a mouse
Ears: Chamois or Ultra Suede
Eyes: Tufts of black crewel yarn
Whiskers: Dark moose body hair

Deer-hair mice have been around for well over half a century and were marketed commercially in the early 1930s. Texan Billy Munn is a respected and talented fly tier specializing in deer-hair bass bugs and he has been instrumental in the development of the Deer-Hair Mouse as it is tied today.

Tied by Tom Farmer

FARMER'S FIELD MOUSE

Hook: Straight eye, wide gape
Tail: Gray Vernille
Body and head: Gray lamb's wool, spun and clipped to shape and coated with clear silicone rubber
Ears: Leather
Eyes: Solid black plastic

Tom Farmer of Dobbs Ferry, New York, is actively involved with the Warm Water Committee of the Federation of Fly Fishers, and is obviously a capable fly tier. Concerning his Field Mouse, Farmer writes that it "was born on the wave of the new silicone-coated flies . . . and not only looks realistic, but will float almost indefinitely."

KATIE'S PET

Hook: Straight eye, wide gape
Tail: Tan-gray Vernille, melted at the end to provide a taper
Legs: Brown rubber hackle, knotted and split to indicate toes
Body: Subtle alternating bands of natural gray and gray dyed tan deer body hair stacked over white hair and clipped to shape
Head and ears: Bands of natural gray and gray dyed tan deer body hair stacked over natural gray hair and clipped to shape
Eyes: Hollow plastic
Whiskers: Fine monofilament

Rubber-hackle legs provide additional action to this appealing deer-hair mouse provided by Kevin McEnerney, a fly tier from the Lake Champlain area of Vermont. McEnerney, who named this fly after his daughter, devotes much of his free time promoting fly tying and fishing to youngsters.

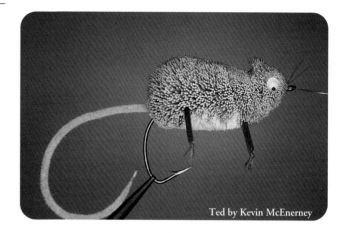

Ted by Kevin McEnerney

MELODY MOUSE

Hook: Straight eye, wide gape
Tail, legs and ears: Tyvec paper, colored and tinted as shown
Body: Gray deer body hair stacked over white deer body hair and trimmed as shown
Eyes: Solid black bead eyes
Whiskers: Fine black elk mane

Tim England tied this little mouse and named it for his wife, Melody. The legs, tail and ears are cut from Tyvec brand paper which is very durable even when wet, and takes color well. The legs extend straight back on either side of the hook and help to stabilize the mouse, acting as outriggers.

Tied by Tim England

WHITLOCK'S MOUSERAT

Hook: Straight eye, wide gape
Tail: Brown chamois strip
Body: Natural dark deer body hair on top (with only the tips of the hair showing and pointing to the rear), stacked over very light gray and natural white deer body hair, trimmed close and flat across the bottom and left entirely untrimmed on top
Ears: Brown chamois, tied in front of the body
Head: Brown dyed deer body hair stacked over natural light grey and white deer body hair, trimmed as shown
Whiskers: Black moose mane or similar, tied back
Eyes: Solid black bead eyes

Dave Whitlock designed this frisky looking mouse for teasing big bass. It is also tied in black.

Tied by Dave Whitlock

Frogs

Tied by Bob Clouser

CLOUSER SIL-E FROG

Hook: Straight eye, wide gape
Legs: Two distinct bunches of gray squirrel tail dyed yellow
Body: Dark olive wool spun, trimmed to shape, and surface coated with clear silicone rubber
Eyes: Flat prismatic peel-off eyes, silver with a black pupil, glued in place and coated with clear silicone rubber

This is an effective yet easy-to-tie frog - perfect for the fly tier who wants to tie his first "silicone fly." Not many people spend more time fly fishing and guiding for bass than Bob Clouser, so when he endorses a fly you can be certain that it works.

Tied by Larry Dahlberg

DAHLBERG FROG DIVER

Hook: Straight eye, wide gape
Legs: On each side a set of two dyed green grizzly hackles inside of which is one yellow hackle. Each set splayed outward
Skirt: Green deer body hair
Collar and head: Green deer body hair, stacked over yellow deer body hair, trimmed to leave a heavy diving collar. Cement the head but not the collar.
Eyes: Solid plastic

This is basically a Dahlberg Diver (which see) tied to resemble a frog. When retrieved, the fly dives below the water's surface and slowly drifts upward between tugs on the line.

Tied by Larry Dahlberg

DAHLBERG SKIPPER FROG

Hook: Straight eye, 3X or 4X long, bent upward about 30 degrees at the mid-point of the shank
Legs: On each side a set of two dyed green grizzly hackles inside of which is a yellow hackle. Each set splayed outward
Skirt: Chartreuse rubber hackle and shorter green rubber hackle
Head: Green deer body hair with a single white stripe stacked over white deer body hair, trimmed into a round nose cylinder, flattened slightly top and bottom, and cemented
Eyes: Large yellow plastic eyes, set high on the top portion of the head

Tied with the hook pointing up, the Skipper Frog won't dig into surface vegetation but is designed to skip and hop on top of weeds and lily pads. Dahlberg says it's deadly, however, when stationary and ". . . the tail feathers slowly settle under the water, right into the face of a following bass, coming to rest in a nearly vertical position with only its eyes and nose peering above the surface. One slurp and it's in his lip."

DAVE'S FROG DIVER

Hook: Straight eye, wide gape

Legs: On each side a set of two dyed olive-green grizzly hackles inside of which is one yellow dyed grizzly hackle, inside of which is one shorter, webby white hackle. Each set splayed outward

Throat: Chartreuse crystal flash

Front legs: A pair each of green, white, black and chartreuse rubber hackle

Collar: Top and sides: A mixture of black and olive deer body hair
Bottom: Chartreuse deer body hair

Diving collar: Black and olive deer body hair, trimmed as shown and cemented over the top only

Head: Alternating spots of olive over black deer body hair stacked over chartreuse and white hair, cemented top and bottom

Eyes: Hollow plastic

This is a great looking diving frog pattern from Dave Whitlock that's deadly on largemouth that are hanging out around the lily pads.

Tied by Dave Whitlock

FARMER'S SILICONE FROG

Hook: Straight eye, wide gape

Legs: The lower legs are strips of olive poly-yarn over yellow poly-yarn with a joint of olive thread; the thigh is olive over yellow lamb's wool. The legs are built on hooks that are one size smaller than the main hook, snipped at the bend and connected with 12 lb. wire at a point about ¼ of an inch up from the "tail."

Forelegs: Olive poly-yarn over yellow poly-yarn with a joint of olive thread

Body: Olive stacked over yellow lamb's wool, shaped, spotted black. Work clear silicone rubber into the feet, thighs and body.

Eyes: Half a hollow plastic eye is glued to the back of an intact hollow plastic eye. The inside eye is painted olive and both sets are cemented into sockets cut into the top of the head.

Note: For a sinking frog, use solid plastic eyes and don't treat the body with silicone rubber.

Tom Farmer says that he ties this pattern without eyes until he decides whether he needs a floating or sinking frog.

Tied by Tom Farmer

MESSINGER BUCKTAIL FROG

Rump: Small bunches of deer body hair, green above and yellow below, applied at the rear and trimmed short before securing the legs

Legs: Green over yellow bucktail is tied on top, in front of the rump, with the tips facing forward. The bucktail is divided into 2 legs and heavy thread is bound to the hook at the leg base and placed within each leg. Knees are formed by inserting a straight pin inside each leg and wrapping a joint over the bucktail, pin and heavy thread. Tie off, bend the knee and cement. Cut away the excess pin. Pulling on the heavy thread will position the legs

Body: Green deer body hair stacked over yellow and white, trimmed as shown with a full, rounded belly

Eyes: Plastic. See Messinger Bucktail Popper Frog on next page

It's hard to imagine how many bass have been caught on a Bucktail Frog created over seventy years ago by Joe Messinger, Sr., of Morgantown, West Virginia. Messinger's design was clearly ahead of its time and we are fortunate to have his tying style perpetuated by his son.

Tied by Joe Messinger, Jr.

Frogs

MESSINGER BUCKTAIL DIVER FROG

Tied by Joe Messinger, Jr.

Hook: Straight eye, wide gape
Legs: Jointed black over green bucktail, tied as described in Messinger Bucktail Frog (page 13)
Diving skirt: Black deer body hair, trimmed as shown, like a Dahlberg Diver, (which see) and well cemented
Body: Green, yellow and black deer body hair stacked over green and white deer body hair, trimmed broad and flat, with a pointed nose
Eyes: Plastic. See Messinger Bucktail Popper Frog below

Joe Messinger, Jr., developed this diving variation of his father's famous Bucktail Frog. He credits Larry Dahlberg for having introduced him to the cemented deer-hair diving head which Messinger incorporated into this frog design.

MESSINGER BUCKTAIL POPPER FROG

Tied by Joe Messinger, Jr.

Hook: Straight eye, wide gape
Legs: Jointed dark brown over yellow bucktail, tied as described in Messinger Bucktail Frog (page 13)
Body: Tan deer body hair stacked over yellow and white deer body hair, trimmed as shown with a cupped popper head formed of body hair and heavily cemented
Eyes: Joe Messinger makes his own eyes by cutting up bits of plastic and dissolving them in acetone. The resulting mush is rolled into balls and glued into the head, shaped while still soft and permitted to dry. After the eyes have hardened they are colored with latex paints, given a black pupil and lacquered

The Bucktail Popper Frog is one of the original designs of Joe Messinger, Sr., dating back to the 1920s.

MESSINGER LEAP FROG

Tied by Joe Messinger, Jr.

Hook: Straight eye, wide gape
Butt: A loop of natural lamb's wool as a support for the skirt and legs
Legs: Two pair of grizzly hackles, dyed yellow, splayed outward
Skirt: Light green deer body hair, with a touch of yellow at the bottom on each side, extending 180 degrees over the top
Body: Light green deer body hair stacked over yellow and white deer body hair and trimmed as shown, leaving enough hair in front on the bottom to form a "lip" that is stiffened with cement
Eyes: Solid plastic

Joe Messinger, Jr., came up with this frog that hops, skips and slides and is fairly easy to tie. As with all the Messinger patterns, other color combinations are often used.

POLYFROG

Hook: Straight eye, wide gape
Underbody: Polypropylene dubbing (or foam) for a floating frog; lead wire for a sinking frog
Body: A thick strand of olive polypropylene yarn over pale yellow (or cream) polypropylene yarn, tied forward then pulled back over the hook and secured at the rear with olive thread
Legs: Divide the olive and pale yellow polypropylene yarn into equal bunches on each side and tie off with olive thread at the knee joint

Allen Eastby introduced these "Poly" bass flies in the early 1980s. He stumbled onto the technique while trying to tie Keith Fulsher's Thunder Creek minnow imitations with polypropylene yarn instead of bucktail. Eastby adapted the "reverse tie" to produce this Polyfrog as well as the following Polywog.

Tied by Jack Russell

POLYWOG

Hook: Standard dry fly or wet fly
Underbody: Poly dubbing or foam for a floater, lead wire for a sinker
Body and tail: Olive polypropylene yarn over pale yellow (or cream) polypropylene yarn, tied forward and pulled back over the hook and secured at the rear with olive thread

Allen Eastby describes this fly as having drawn its inspiration from a New Zealand pattern. He ties the Polywog in a variety of colors and sizes including ". . . large ones which provoke especially savage responses from largemouth bass."

Tied by Jack Russell

POP LIPS FROG

Hook: Straight eye, wide gape
Legs: Greenish yellow lamb's wool, divided into two legs, darkened on top with a green marker and striped with a black marker
Feet and toes: The lamb's wool legs are tied off with green thread wraps to form a leg joint, then divided into toes, held in place with clear silicone rubber
Body and head: Greenish yellow lamb's wool, trimmed leaving a heavy "bib" or beard of wool in front. Clear silicone rubber is spread over the wool, and the lip is shaped almost flat and trimmed as shown
Eyes: Formed when applying the silicone to the head and colored with marking pens

This is Bob Popovics' design of a silicone-bodied swimming frog. With a little bit of experimentation with the silicone lip you can probably get this fly to do everything but mate.

Tied by Bob Popovics

Frogs

Tied by Peter Sang

SANG FROG

Hook: Straight eye, wide gape or salmon dry fly
Butt: Yellow deer body hair spun and clipped into a ball
Legs: Green rubber hackle, knotted and separated into toes
Underbody: Closed cell foam, built up for additional bulk
Body: Light yellow chenille
Head: Green deer body hair, spun and clipped flat on the top and bottom leaving some longer strands on the sides to represent front legs
Eyes: Hollow plastic

Peter Sang, an attorney from Portland, Maine, conceived this uncomplicated-yet-effective frog pattern in about 1985. Sang described his frog as "barely" floating with its head just above the surface and its legs and body dangling down "like a real frog."

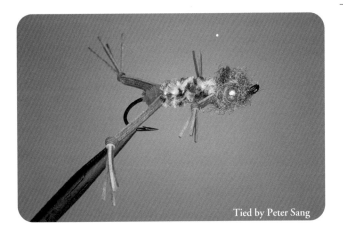

Tied by Peter Sang

SANG SINKING FROG

Hook: Salmon dry fly or low-water
Butt: Red chenille
Legs: Green rubber hackle, knotted and separated into toes
Body: Yellow and black variegated chenille
Forelegs: Green rubber hackle, tied short with knotted joints and separated into toes
Eyes: Gold bead chain
Head: Olive dubbing

Peter Sang's first Sang Sinking Frog was tied without forelegs or a dubbed head. Sang now feels that these additions greatly improve the underwater appearance and swimming action of this fly. This easy-to-tie frog is one you might experiment with at your favorite pond.

Tied by Jim Stewart

STEWART'S DANCING FROG

Hook: Straight eye, wide gape
Tail: Yellow and green rubber hackle
Body: Deer body hair in several shades of green with black spots stacked over yellow deer body hair, trimmed to shape and cemented on the popping surface and bottom
Eyes: Solid plastic

Jim Stewart designed this fly to resemble a floating Hula Popper, the famous bass lure for both spinning and casting. An architect from Tampa, Florida, Stewart has the opportunity to perfect his fly designs on some pretty big largemouth bass.

STEWART'S HAIR SPOON FROG

Hook: Straight eye, wide gape
Tail: Chartreuse rubber hackle
Body: Deer body hair in several shades of green, with black spots, stacked over yellow and trimmed flat on bottom as shown. It is cemented in front and on the bottom. Viewed from above this fly has a fat tear-drop, or spoon-like shape from which it derives its name
Eyes: Solid plastic

Jim Stewart's Hair Spoon Frog should be fished very slowly across the tops of lily pads. Once it reaches open water, a sharp pull will make it dive so it can then be fished back below the surface.

Tied by Jim Stewart

WHITLOCK'S NEAR NUFF FROG

Hook: Straight eye, wide gape
Legs: On each side a set of one natural grizzly hackle, outside of which is one dyed yellow grizzly hackle, outside of which is one dyed olive grizzly hackle. Each set is splayed outward
Skirt: Olive grizzly hackle
Body: Yellow, olive and black dyed deer body hair, stacked over white and trimmed to shape
Eyes: Hollow plastic

Billy Munn of Bridgeport, Texas, tied this well-known Dave Whitlock fly and suggests fishing it with a sink-tip line which causes the frog to dive when retrieved. When the line goes slack, the frog floats back to the surface. Munn says that most strikes seem to occur just as the frog breaks the surface.

Tied by Billy Munn

WHITLOCK'S WIGGLELEGS FROG

Legs: Onto a straight-eyed hook tie on a grizzly hackle dyed yellow, then bunches of green and white (deer rump hair) or bucktail, all with the tips facing forward. Wrap thread to the rear and pull the hair and hackle back over the hook, maintaining separation. Thread wraps form an ankle joint. Cut off the remainder of the hook behind the ankle, cement and set aside to dry. Both legs will be attached to the main hook using loops of .010 - .014 inch wire after the first bunches of body hair have been applied
Body: Deer body hair: dark green with black stripes stacked over olive and white, trimmed as shown and cemented on bottom
Forelegs: Three or four knotted white rubber hackles tied in about ¾ way up the body, divided into feet below the knots
Eyes: Hollow plastic

Dave Whitlock introduced this cleverly-constructed frog in the 1975 edition of *The Fly-Tyers Almanac*. He suggests not treating it with flotant so it will ride low in the water like a live frog.

Tied by Umpqua Feather Merchants

Crayfish

Tied by Don Brown

BROWN'S CRAYFISH

Hook:	Down eye, 1X long
Claws:	Red squirrel tail, divided
Body:	Dark brown yarn or chenille
Legs:	Soft brown or furnace hackle, tied in by the tip, palmered forward and pulled down with the greatest concentration of wraps near the eye of the hook
Shellback:	Dyed brown goose quill, pulled forward over the body and coated with several coats of polyurethane varnish

An underbody of lead wire is always an option for keeping a crayfish or any fly near the bottom in fast water. Don Brown, who developed this fly, suggests using lead very sparingly or not at all because it inhibits the natural movement of the fly. He furthermore says that his crayfish has taken many good bass when fished on the surface.

CLAY'S CRAYFISH

Tied by Tim England

Hook:	Salmon double
Nose:	Gray squirrel body hair dyed purple
Antennae:	Fine black elk mane
Eyes:	25 lb. monofilament dipped in black lacquer and epoxy
Claws:	Gray squirrel tail dyed purple
Underbody:	Twiston flat lead strip
Thorax:	Heavy white chenille, the first turn taken ahead of the pincers
Legs:	Grizzly hackle dyed purple, palmered over the thorax and trimmed top and bottom
Abdomen:	Medium white chenille
Rib:	Clear monofilament
Carapace:	Gray squirrel tail dyed purple, ribbed over the thorax with monofilament and saturated with rubber cement
Tail:	Gray squirrel tail dyed purple, shaped with rubber cement
Note:	The carapace and tail are coated with two part epoxy rod varnish

Tim England first tied this pattern around 1975, and he ties it in many colors.

CLOUSER CRAYFISH

Tied by Bob Clouser

Hook:	Down eye, 3X or 4X long
Underbody:	Lead wire mounted on each side of the hook shank
Antennae:	A small bunch of ringneck cock pheasant tail feather barbs
Nose:	Tip of a hen mallard flank feather on top of the antennae
Claws:	Hen mallard, cut to shape
Body:	Pale gray yarn
Legs:	Grizzly hackle, bleached ginger
Head, back and tail:	Olive Furry Foam
Rib:	Gray thread

Bob Clouser of Middletown, Pennsylvania, is one of the most influential and respected bass-fly tiers and guides in the east. The popular Clouser Crayfish was designed for river smallmouth and is a fine example of how Clouser applies his fishing experience to fly design.

CRAWDAD SHEDDER

Hook:	Down eye, 4X to 6X long
Claws:	Deer body hair, divided
Underbody:	Lead wire, or wool if additional weight is not wanted
Body:	Tan chenille
Tail:	Dark deer body hair

Pennsylvania fly tier and outdoor writer Ed Howey once wrote that most crayfish patterns "... simply demand too much time at the vise ... I've come to rely on a simple pattern using but two materials: chenille and deer hair." His Crawdad Shedder imitates a crayfish during a period of molt when their colors are lighter and when they are most vulnerable.

Tied by Dick Stewart

POP LIPS CRAYFISH

Hook: Straight eye, 4X long, wide gape
Eyes: Melted monofilament
Claws: Olive over light tan lamb's wool
Thorax and abdomen: Green lamb's wool on top and light tan wool on the bottom, trimmed to shape, leaving a beard of wool below the hook eye from which to build the tail and diving lip

Nose, carapace and tail: Clear silicone rubber
Note: Once the fly has been completed and the tail (diving lip) has been trimmed to shape, the underbody may be colored with marking pens to match the mottled and varied colors of natural crayfish.

Bob Popovics of Seaside, New Jersey, pioneered the development of silicone flies - first for saltwater, now for bass. His lip design adds significantly to the fly's action.

Tied by Bob Popovics

ROBINSON'S MUD BUG

Hook: Wilson dry salmon, slightly bent
Antennae: Orange rubber hackle
Eyes: Melted monofilament
Weight: Flattened dumbbell lead eyes, tied in underneath, behind hook eye
Thorax underbody: Dense foam, trimmed oval, slit lengthwise and secured onto the underside of the hook
Thorax and abdomen: Orange Antron
Claws: A piece of shaped Ultra Suede pulled through a slit made in the foam underbody

Carapace and tail: Orange Ultra Suede, cut to shape and cemented to the body and ribbed with copper wire, defining segments. The tail is then folded over the hook eye and cemented underneath to the flattened lead eyes
Legs: Orange rubber hackle threaded through with a large needle
Note: Further detailing may be applied with a waterproof marking pen.

Tied by Joe Robinson

SWIMMING CRAYFISH

Hook: Salmon wet, Bartleet
Underbody: Lead wire over the front ⅔ of the hook shank
Antennae: Ringneck pheasant tail barbs. (At this point tie in 2 bunches of natural brown bucktail; bunch #1 facing forward over the antennae; bunch #2 in opposite direction)
Claws: Tan bucktail, divided

Abdomen & thorax: Tan chenille
Legs: Ringneck pheasant body feather tied flat above thorax
Tail and carapace: Fold bunch #1 over legs, tie off behind thorax. Fold ½ of bunch #2 over abdomen, rib with tan thread and tie off. Trim balance of bunch #2 to form tail.

Byron Yarrington tied this pattern to imitate a fleeing crayfish. It should be tied and fished with this in mind.

Tied by Byron Yarrington

WHITLOCK'S SOFTSHELL CRAYFISH

Hook: Down eye, 6X long
Claws: Matched hen body feathers
Eyes: Melted monofilament
Antennae: Black rubber hackle (or peccary)
Nose: Nylon raffia (or short bunch of ruddy elk or deer body hair)
Thorax: Golden yellow dubbing
Legs: Soft grizzly hackle, dyed yellow and trimmed on the bottom
Abdomen: Golden yellow dubbing

Rib: Silver (or copper) wire
Carapace and tail: Red-brown nylon raffia, tied in behind the claws, pulled over the thorax, ribbed over the abdomen with the wire, and detailed with a black marker
Note: Weight may be added by tying in lead eyes behind the hook eye and masking them with matching color dubbing and paint.

This Dave Whitlock crayfish imitation is tied in a variety of convincing color combinations. It rides upside-down to reduce fouling on weeds.

Tied by Umpqua Feather Merchants

Leeches

Tied by Doug Tucker-Eccher

Tied by Tom Nixon

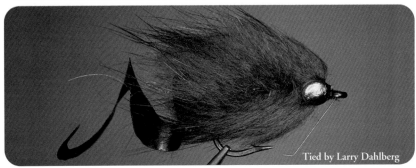

Tied by Larry Dahlberg

CURL-TAIL LEECH

Hook: Straight eye, wide gape
Tail: Blue crystal flash over which is a piece of natural or imitation chamois dyed blue and cut as shown
Body: Black crystal chenille
Hackle: Long black saddle, tied in by the tip and palmered over the body with the fluff at the base left on the stem, forming a marabou-like collar

Doug Tucker-Eccher, of The Bass Pond ties this fly for his shop in this and other color combinations including black with a chartreuse tail; purple with a fluorescent red tail; and solid black or purple.

FUR LEECH

Hook: Straight eye, wide gape
Tail: Black rabbit fur strip, skin side up
Body: Cross-cut black rabbit fur strip, wrapped over the full length of the hook shank
Eyes: Silver bead chain or chrome lead eyes with black pupils

Nothing looks quite as alive and slimy as a wet rabbit-fur-strip leech being drawn slowly through the water. With every movement of the rod tip, every pull on the line, and Tom Nixon's Fur Leech dances and shivers with life.

LARRY'S LEECH

Hook: Straight eye, short shank, heavy wire
Tail: Brown latex cut into a spiral shape
Body: Natural dark brown rabbit fur strip wrapped over the full length of the hook shank
Head: Chrome lead eyes

When Larry Dahlberg first fished with Dave Whitlock, he was shown Whitlock's Chamois Leech. Dahlberg liked the idea of the fly but set out to develop a fly using latex instead of chamois. Cut into a spiral shape, the latex tail creates a lot of action with a normal retrieve.

Tied by Dick Stewart

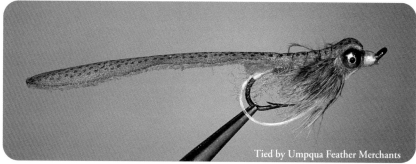

Tied by Umpqua Feather Merchants

Tied by Umpqua Feather Merchants

THOM GREEN LEECH

Hook: 4X long, bent upward as shown
Underbody: Lead wire, on the rear section of the bent hook shank
Tail: Black marabou
Body: Black yarn or dubbing
Collar: Soft black hackle
Note: This leech is also tied in claret, brown or olive.

This is an easy leech to tie but don't be fooled, it has accounted for many bass in both the far north and deep south. A favorite way to fish leeches is to cast toward the shoreline and slowly swim the fly into deeper water, maintaining its position just inches off the bottom.

WHITLOCK'S CHAMOIS LEECH

Hook: Salmon wet
Underbody: Lead wire
Tail support: Red polypropylene yarn
Body: Brown dubbing
Throat: Brown speckled hen body or similar feather
Eyes: Silver bead chain
Rib: Monofilament
Back and tail: Chamois strip, tied in at the front, pulled over the eyes and secured to the body with the monofilament rib, then freckled with a black marking pen

Tan, olive and black are other popular color combinations for this fly.

WHITLOCK'S 'LECTRIC LEECH

Hook: Salmon wet
Tail: Black marabou, over which is peacock herl with strands of pearl or blue Flashabou on each side (make certain that the Flashabou and peacock herl are long enough to pull forward)
Body: Black yarn or dubbing with remaining Flashabou pulled forward along each side and the peacock herl brought over the top
Hackle: Black schlappen or hackle palmered forward over the body, the Flashabou and the peacock herl
Head: Black with a band of Flashabou

This design by Dave Whitlock has lots of motion and shows a bit of flash.

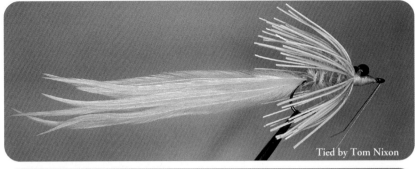

Tied by Tom Nixon

Tied by Kevin McEnerney

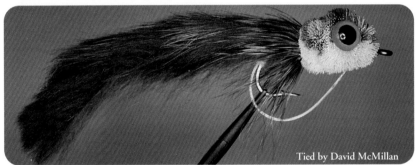

Tied by David McMillan

ALBINO SERPENT

Hook: Straight eye, heavy wire
Tail: 6 to 8 long, narrow white or cream saddle hackles
Body: Light blue chenille
Body hackle: Palmered white or cream
Collar: White rubber hackle
Head: White
Eyes: Gold (plastic) bead chain with painted black pupils or similar

Tom Nixon designed this fly for fishing in "shallow vegetation and heavy timber cover." The extra long hackles and rubber collar provide this shallow-running fly with everything a bass could want. Note the wire weed guard favored by Nixon.

EEL

Hook: Straight eye, wide gape
Tail support: Loop of stiff monofilament
Underbody: Soft round lead wire or "Led" covered with thread and cemented
Tail: Flat latex, cut in a spiral shape and colored with waterproof marking pens
Body: Strip of natural latex, wound over the lead base and colored with waterproof marking pens as shown

Kevin McEnerney designed this pattern to provide a lot of natural movement in the water. McEnerney lives in Vermont and fishes primarily in the Lake Champlain basin where the Eel is his best fly for both largemouth and smallmouth bass.

McEELWORM

Hook: Straight eye, heavy wire, stainless
Tail: Olive rabbit fur strip
Skirt: Olive grizzly hackle
Head: Yellow, olive, light olive and dyed brown deer body hair stacked over natural white deer body hair and sculpted with a furrow between the recessed eyes as shown
Eyes: Solid plastic, red with a black pupil

David McMillan of Fort Worth, Texas, likes to go after really big "double digit" bass as he describes them. The heads of his flies are carefully sculpted to ". . . look mean, in hopes of triggering an aggressive predatorial response" rather than a hard-to-detect gentle pick up.

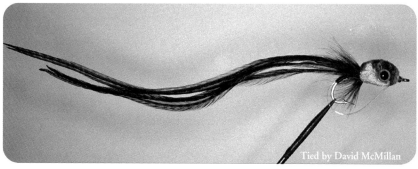

Tied by David McMillan

Tied by Jim Stewart

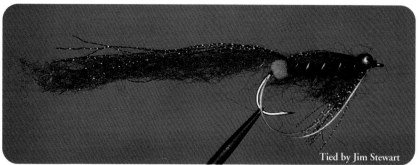

Tied by Jim Stewart

McSNAKE

Hook:	Straight eye, heavy wire, stainless
Tail:	Four extra long, narrow grizzly saddle hackles dyed brown
Skirt:	Soft grizzly hackle dyed olive
Head:	Gray, yellow and dyed brown deer body hair stacked in alternating bands over natural white as illustrated, and trimmed into a snake-like flat wedge shape
Eyes:	Solid plastic, red with a black pupil, set into deep sockets

Developed by David McMillan of Fort Worth, Texas. McMillan is a proponent of fishing a floating fly on a sinking line, a technique he uses to keep his fly deep, yet suspended above underwater vegetation. Control over depth is achieved by adjusting the length of the leader. This fly is over 8 inches long.

STEWART'S FUZZY WUZZY

Hook:	Straight eye, wide gape
Butt:	A double loop or two of heavy red yarn as a tail support
Tail:	Yellow over which is white Icelandic wool (streamer hair) over which is mixed lime and silver crystal flash
Skirt:	Red crystal flash on the bottom only
Body:	Light brown bear hair and yellow calftail blended with smaller amounts of red and purple calftail, dubbed with a spinning loop, and picked out
Legs:	Orange rubber hackle on the sides
Head:	Fluorescent orange thread
Eyes:	Chrome-plated plastic bead chain

Jim Stewart designed the Fuzzy Wuzzy to be fished very slowly over the tops of weed beds "…slightly twitched to cause the tail to be very active with minimum movement forward."

STEWART'S RATTLE WORM

Hook:	Straight eye, wide gape
Rattle:	A glass worm rattle, secured to the underside of the hook with the tapered end towards the hook eye
Butt:	Fluorescent pink chenille
Tail and shellback:	Red-brown combed (polyolifin) needlecraft yarn over which is peacock crystal flash (leave enough material to pull forward for shellback and throat)
Body:	Black Leech Yarn, picked out
Rib:	Oval gold tinsel
Eyes:	Gold bead chain
Throat:	The yarn and crystal flash is pulled over the eyes, tied down and pulled underneath to form the throat

The Rattle Worm is a noise-making fly that was tied to be fished in the same way a rigged plastic worm is fished - on the bottom and *very* slowly.

Tied by Tom Farmer

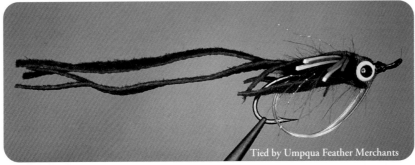

Tied by Umpqua Feather Merchants

Tied by Farrow Allen

WATER MOCCASIN

Hook: Straight eye, wide gape
Tail: Black rabbit fur strip, fur side down, with pieces of floating foam glued at intervals on the skin side
Collar: Black hackle, heavily wound
Head: Black spun deer body hair or lamb's wool trimmed flat as shown with the nose curving up slightly like the tip of a ski. If deer hair is used, it should be lightly coated with a vinyl cement; if wool is used the head should be treated with clear silicone rubber
Eyes: Hollow or solid plastic, glued on top
Note: For additional movement experiment by using less foam or nicking the hide to develop hinge points.

This floating water snake imitation was developed by Tom Farmer for largemouth bass.

WHITLOCK'S CHAMOIS LIZARD

Hook: Salmon wet
Legs: Sparse pearl crystal flash, white and black rubber hackle
Body: Black fur
Eyes: Solid plastic
Back: Long black chamois strip, split as shown, tied in at the head and cemented to the top of the body
Belly: Short black chamois strip cut into a "V" around the hook point and cemented to the underside of the body

Aquatic lizards and salamanders have never been known as important baits, yet Dave Whitlock's fork-tailed Chamois Lizard, fished slowly on the bottom, draws a lot of attention from cruising bass.

WHITLOCK'S EELWORM STREAMER

Hook: Salmon wet
Wing: 4 long, narrow yellow-dyed grizzly hackles outside of which are 2 short, wide yellow-dyed grizzly hackles
Eyes: Chromed lead or silver bead chain, tied under hook shank
Body: Black chenille or dubbing
Hackle: Yellow-dyed grizzly, palmered over the chenille
Head: Red

Dave Whitlock introduced his now well-known Eelworm in the *Fly Tyer's Almanac* that he and Robert H. Boyle published in 1975. He described it then as ". . . a fly-rodder's answer to the plastic worm . . . without a doubt the most effective largemouth bass streamer I've ever used for bass living in reservoirs and natural lakes." Tie this in your favorite colors.

Tied by Umpqua Feather Merchants

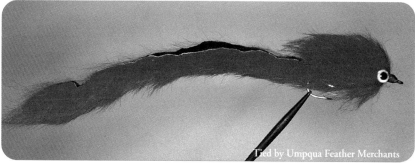

Tied by Umpqua Feather Merchants

Tied by Dave Whitlock

WHITLOCK'S HARE WATERPUP

Hook: Salmon wet
Body: Black fur
Wing: Black rabbit fur strip, tied in at the head, glued and secured to the body with copper wire, matuka style
Throat: Red Flashabou
Collar: Black deer body hair
Head: Black deer body hair, trimmed fairly flat on the top and bottom and cemented
Eyes: Hollow plastic

Waterpups (or waterdogs) are the immature stage of terrestrial salamanders found in some parts of the country. They are a common forage for bass.

WHITLOCK'S HARE WORM

Hook: Straight eye, wide gape
Wing: Long claret rabbit fur strip impaled over the hook point - skin side up - the forward end secured under the hook shank, behind the hook eye
Back: A short strip of claret rabbit-fur strip, skinside down, cemented on top and secured behind the eye of the hook
Eyes: Solid plastic

Several of Dave Whitlock's newer fly creations utilize rabbit-fur strips that wave and flutter as the fly is retreived. The Hare Worm is usually fished at intermediate depths whereas Whitlock's Hare Diver is intended for use at the surface, and Whitlock's Hare Jig is designed to sink quickly and may be bounced off the bottom.

WHITLOCK'S WATER SNAKE DIVER

Hook: Straight eye, wide gape
Wing: Red-brown rabbit fur strip and with black stripes applied with a marking pen
Skirt: Red-brown deer body hair, on the top only
Diving collar: Red-brown deer body hair, trimmed short on top only
Head: Red-brown deer body hair stacked over pale yellow, trimmed flat and slightly rounded as shown to have the appearance of a snake's head (The black stripes on top and lateral line on the side of the head are applied with a marking pen)
Eyes: Solid plastic

Smaller water snakes can be very attractive to a hungry bass.

Divers

Tied by Ed Rief

Tied by Pierre Saumur

Tied by Larry Dahlberg

BULLET BUG

Hook: Straight eye, wide gape
Tail: Sparse olive marabou and peacock herl over which is pearlescent yellow crystal flash, outside of which are 2 olive dyed grizzly hackles, splayed
Body: Pearlescent Mylar tubing with the ends unravelled, trailing behind
Head and collar: Olive and black deer body hair, spun and trimmed as a diver, cemented on bottom
Note: Also popular tied in other colors and with varying head sizes.

The Bullet Bug was developed by Ed Rief of Eddies' Flies in Bangor, Maine. Rief lives only a few blocks from the famed Bangor Salmon Pool on the Penobscot River, but he is best known for his passionate pursuit of smallmouth bass in the upper river.

CHANTIÈRE

Hook: Straight eye, wide gape
Tail: Yellow rubber hackle and two dyed purple hen body feathers or similar, splayed out
Skirt: Purple deer body hair
Legs: White, green and purple rubber hackle
Body: Purple, mustard and white deer body hair spun and trimmed as shown
Head: Pale green bullet head and collar, well cemented
Forelegs: White and purple rubber hackle secured with fluorescent green thread used in making the bullet head
Eyes: Painted yellow with a black pupil

This is an unique bullet-head diving fly from Pierre Saumur of Montreal, Quebec.

DAHLBERG DIVER (ORIGINAL)

Hook: Straight eye, heavy wire
Tail: 50 or more strands of gold Flashabou; over which is white and brown marabou
Collar and head: Brown deer body hair clipped to shape and cemented on bottom

Larry Dahlberg developed his now well-known diver while experimenting with Flashabou and its application to surface flies. After figuring how to make his fly dive, swim and resurface properly, he encountered a problem he hadn't anticipated, he couldn't get any of his clients to fish it. "It looked so odd . . . traditionalists wouldn't even tie it to their leader!" Today the Dahlberg Diver, in many forms, can be found on bass waters from coast to coast.

Tied by Larry Dahlberg

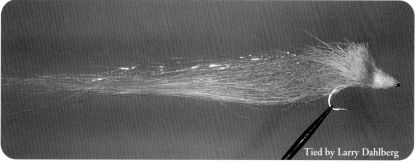

Tied by Larry Dahlberg

Tied by Jim Stewart

DAHLBERG FUR-STRIP DIVER

Hook: Straight eye, heavy wire
Tail: Tapered white rabbit fur strip over which are a few strands of light blue Flashabou
Body: Cross-cut rabbit fur strip, palmered and trimmed flush across the bottom
Skirt: Natural white deer body hair
Head and collar: Natural white deer body hair spun and trimmed to form a diving collar and head, well cemented on the bottom only

The Fur Strip Diver is a variation of the "original" Dahlberg Diver. Dahlberg emphasizes that "It's important on all of these divers that the tail be extra long . . . because the vortex created by the diving head will pull a short tail up tight behind the collar when the fly is retrieved."

DAHLBERG MEGA-DIVER

Hook: Straight eye, heavy wire, stainless
Tail: White Hairabou, teased over which is a sparse mixture of pearl Flashabou and crystal hair, all quite long
Skirt: Natural white deer body hair
Collar and head: Natural white deer body hair, spun and trimmed as a diver and cemented on the bottom

The Dahlberg Mega-Diver was originally developed for northern pike and uses teased synthetic hair to produce a very large fly that will cast well, even into a stiff breeze. To cast this fly, which is over 8 inches long, Dahlberg uses a 9 foot rod with a 7-weight line at an average casting distance of 80 feet.

STEWART'S BASS-A-ROO

Hook: Straight eye, wide gape
Tail: Orange bucktail over which is yellow bucktail over which are three pairs of grizzly hackles dyed yellow, splayed out, over which is gold Flashabou and pearlescent yellow crystal flash
Butt: Fluorescent orange chenille
Gills: Fluorescent red marabou on each side
Skirt: Pale yellow on the side and dark yellow on top
Body: Dark and pale yellow deer body hair stacked over light fluorescent orange and trimmed to shape as shown and cemented in front and on the bottom
Eyes: Solid plastic

The Bass-a-roo was designed by Jim Stewart to dive when retrieved and pop back to the surface at rest. On a steady retrieve it swims fairly deep.

Tied by Jim Stewart

Tied by Tim England

Tied by Dave Whitlock

STEWART'S LUCKY WIGGLER

Hook: Straight eye, wide gape
Tail: White, orange and green rubber hackle over which are six broad yellow grizzly hackles, splayed out over which is gold Flashabou and yellow pearlescent crystal flash on top
Butt: Fluorescent orange chenille
Skirt: Chartreuse spun deer body hair, clipped at the bottom to expose the butt
Body: Stacked chartreuse, white and orange deer body hair trimmed as shown and cemented front and bottom
Eyes: Solid plastic

Designed by Jim Stewart of Tampa, Florida, the Lucky Wiggler leaves a long stream of bubbles on a diving retrieve.

TY'S TANTALIZER (IMPROVED)

Hook: Straight eye, wide gape
Tail: Full yellow marabou, on each side a cree hackle splayed out and down, and yellow pearlescent crystal flash
Collar: Dark brown on top of light brown over yellow deer body hair
Head: Dark brown and light brown deer body hair stacked over yellow; red at the head, trimmed as shown
Note: In the original pattern the deer hair diving lip extended beyond the hook eye and completely obscured it. The leader was attached to a loop of heavy monofilament secured to the hook shank so that it protruded up from the middle of the flat diving lip.

Tim England's original version was replaced by the improved version in the late 1980s. The original dives a bit deeper.

WHITLOCK'S HARE DIVER

Hook: Salmon wet
Tail and body: Pale yellow synthetic yarn
Wing: Olive rabbit fur strip, tied in at the head and cemented to the top of the body, outside of which on either side is a short section of pearlescent green crystal flash
Pectoral fins: Olive dyed grizzly hen hackles
Legs: Black rubber hackle and chartreuse Speckle Flake rubber hackle
Collar: Top: Deer body hair dyed dark olive
Bottom: Cream deer body hair
Head: Dark olive deer body hair stacked over cream deer body hair; trimmed flat on the bottom and cemented, trimmed longer on the top, cemented, smoothed back and flattened
Eyes: Solid plastic, small

BRASS HARE

Hook: Straight eye, light wire
Head: Brass bead, slid over the hook and up to the eye
Tail: Blue-dyed rabbit fur strip, skin side up
Body: Cross-cut blue rabbit fur strip wound forward to the head
Collar: Blue and black rubber hackle

Tim England began tying his brass bead-head jig patterns in the mid 1970s. Unlike lead-head jigs that fish well but cast poorly, England's low density brass-head jigs cast easily and fish just like the heavier lead-head jigs.

Tied by Tim England

EGG SUCKING JIG LEECH

Hook: 1/32 to 1/16 oz. lead jig head
Jig head: Painted fluorescent red, orange, green or yellow
Tail: Black marabou
Body: Black chenille
Hackle: Black schlappen
Note: Although the possible combinations of colors is limitless, an all black tail, body and hackle with a the head painted in any of the fluorescent colors is hard to top.

For Pacific salmon and steelhead the Egg Sucking Leech has become popular on the west coast and in Alaska. Using a painted lead head to imitate the egg, this jig is deadly on bass and panfish.

Tied by Karl Svendsen

HOLSCHLAG HACKLE FLY

Hook: 1/32 oz. lead jig head (#2 hook)
Tail: Brown marabou, tied quite full. Gold crystal flash can be included to increase the visibility in clouded water
Body: Brown chenille
Hackle: Brown, palmered over the body
Legs: Yellow rubber hackle
Head: Red or brown painted head with eye

Tim Holschlag, author of *Stream Smallmouth Fishing* designed this pattern exclusively for midwestern smallmouth bass in moving water. If you can't find the right weight jig head, lead "dumbbell" eyes can be used to achieve good results.

Tied by Tim Holschlag

WHITLOCK'S HARE JIG FLY

Hook: Straight eye, wide gape, bent down
Legs: Black rubber hackle with red and pearl crystal flash
Eyes: Lead, painted white with fluorescent red pupils
Wing: A long black rabbit fur strip, skin side up, threaded over the hook point, brought forward under the hook and secured at the head. On top, a short piece of black rabbit fur strip long enough to cover the hook shank and cemented to the rabbit strip below, sandwiching the legs and hook shank between the upper and lower fur strips

This new Jig Fly from Dave Whitlock has the ability to dredge bass up from the depths. Using lead eyes to create a jig permits Whitlock to fine tune his fly and use as much or as little weight as needed.

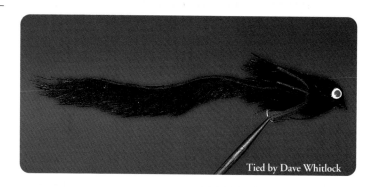

Tied by Dave Whitlock

Tied by Eric Leiser

ANGUS (BLACK)

Hook: Straight eye, heavy wire
Tail: Two pairs of black hackles curving out
Underbody: Heavy lead wire on the forward ⅝ of the hook shank
Body: Black floss
Hackle: About five full black marabou plumes, palmered over the floss, with several strands of black or pearl crystal flash tied in before the last one or two marabou plumes are wrapped
Head and collar: Black, interspersed with a sparse red deer body hair and a few strands of black or pearl crystal flash, spun and trimmed into a flattened, pointed wedge as shown

Designed by Eric Leiser for Alaskan rainbow trout after Angus Cameron asked for him for a fly that was ". . . something like a Woolly Bugger, a Muddler and a leech." The Angus has proved itself a very good fly with many gamefish, including bass, and it can be tied in any desired color combination.

Tied by Tom Nixon

BADGER STREAMER

Hook: Down eye, 4X to 6X long
Tail: White bucktail or white goose wing quill section
Body: Silver tinsel chenille, tied full
Wing: Four badger hackles or two badger hackles outside of two olive hackles
Shoulder: A section of barred woodduck
Throat: Orange hackle (optional)

Tom Nixon has referred to the Badger Streamer as ". . . basically a moving water fly" for New England's "slab-sided smallmouth." Nonetheless, it has proven itself as a worthy contender for bass in Kentucky and Louisiana.

Tied by Ed Rief

BANDY-LEGGED MUDDLER

Hook: Down eye, 3X or 4X long
Tail: Orange rubber hackle
Body: Pearlescent Mylar wrapped over orange thread
Wing: Orange marabou over which is peacock herl
Collar: Rusty orange deer body hair, trimmed away on the bottom to expose the body
Head: Rusty orange deer body hair, spun and clipped as shown and cemented on the bottom
Note: Popular variations are white, yellow and chartreuse. A larger head may be constructed if more surface commotion is desired.

Developed for smallmouth fishing by Ed Rief of Eddie's Flies in Bangor, Maine. Although Maine is most often thought of as a center for trout and salmon fishing - which it is - the Pine Tree State also supports some of the best smallmouth bass fishing in the east.

BASS BUDDY

Hook: Down eye, 6X long
Body: White floss
Rib: Flat silver tinsel
Wing: A pair of white hackles outside of which are yellow hackles
Throat: Red hackle barbs
Cheeks: Dyed red breast hackle over which is a jungle cock eye or substitute

Sometimes tied on a short, straight-eye hook, this bright, traditionally-constructed streamer was developed by J.M Stott and introduced in A.D. Livingston's 1977 book *Tying Bugs and Flies for Bass*.

Tied by Farrow Allen

BASS BUGGER (PURPLE AND PINK)

Hook: Straight eye, heavy wire
Tail: Pink marabou mixed with pink crystal flash
Body: Purple crystal chenille
Hackle: Long purple saddle, tied in by the tip and palmered over the body with the fluff at the base left on the stem, forming a marabou collar
Legs: Three pairs of long pink round rubber hackles, tied in about mid body
Eyes: Lead, with red prismatic peel-off stick-on Lure Eyes

This Woolly Bugger-type fly was developed by Doug Tucker-Eccher of The Bass Pond, a fly-fishing shop in Littleton, Colorado. Tucker-Eccher ties the Bass Bugger with very long rubber hackle in a variety of colors including brown and orange; black and blue; and black and chartreuse.

Tied by Doug Tucker-Eccher

BETTS' BULL-IT HEAD (BASS FRY)

Hook: Kinked shank popper hook
Weight: .025 lead wire, secured on the bend of the hook with Super Glue after the fly has been completed
Diving lip: .010 clear Mylar, cut to shape
Tail: Clear Z-Lon, tinted on the end with olive marking pen
Body: Closed-cell foam (Evasote) colored with olive and yellow marking pens
Eyes: Steel or brass plated black-headed stainless steel dressmaker pins, pushed into the foam body, and trimmed
Note: A description for making the diving lip and the foam body can be found on page 2 under Betts' Bull-it Head Flashdancer.

This realistic bass-fry minnow is part of John Betts' Bull-it Head series. Within the Bull-it Head style it is possible to create all sorts of minnows if you have a good imagination and an adequate supply of waterproof marking pens.

Tied by John Betts

Baitfish

Tied by Farrow Allen

BLACK GHOST MARABOU

Hook: Down eye, 4X to 6X long
Tail: A small bunch of yellow hackle barbs
Body: Black floss or yarn, applied heavily
Rib: Flat silver tinsel
Throat: Yellow hackle barbs
Wing: White marabou
Cheeks: Jungle cock (optional)

The Black Ghost was developed in Maine during the 1920s for landlocked salmon and brook trout. Originally it was tied with narrow saddle-hackle wings. Dressed with a full marabou wing, the Black Ghost is a productive baitfish imitation for bass in still or moving water.

Tied by Dick Stewart

BLACK NOSE DACE

Hook: Down eye, 4X to 6X long
Tail: Red yarn, short
Body: Flat silver tinsel
Rib: Oval silver tinsel
Wing: A small bunch of white bucktail over which is a small bunch of black bear or skunk hair over which is natural brown bucktail
Note: Silver Mylar tubing secured with red tying thread is often substituted for the tinsel body and red wool tail

Originated in New York State by Catskill fly tier Art Flick who introduced the Black Nose Dace as a trout fly in his 1947 book *Streamside Guide to Naturals and Their Imitations*. For trout or bass this is clearly one of the most realistic dace imitations in use.

Tied by Sheldon Bolstad

BOLSTAD SKIPPING MINNOW

Hook: Kinked shank popper hook or straight eye, 3X long
Tail: Red marabou
Underbody: Closed-cell foam, built up
Body: Pearl Flashabou Minnow Body tubing, coated with epoxy
Eyes: Hollow plastic

Sheldon Bolstad's Skipping Minnow was orginally tied to imitate shad fleeing across the surface, trying to get away from pursuing schools of white bass. Bolstad has found that his Skipping Minnow works equally well on surface-feeding smallmouth.

BOLSTAD SPUTTER MINNOW

Hook: Straight eye popper hook, 3X long, with the barb pinched down
           to accommodate the spinner blade and bead
Head: Spinner blade, followed by a clear glass bead, secured in place
Tail: Red marabou
Underbody: Closed-cell foam, built up
Body: Blacktone Flashabou Minnow Body tubing, coated with epoxy
Eyes: Hollow plastic

The addition of a spinner blade at the head of this floating minnow makes
it easy to create a fuss and kick up a lot spray without actually moving the
fly away from prime cover.

Tied by Sheldon Bolstad

BRISTLEBACK

Hook: Down eye, 4X long
Underbody: Lead wire
Body: White chenille
Wing and tail: Two webby fluorescent green neck hackles
Back: Two pieces of fine black chenille
Head: Fluorescent green with painted white eyes with black pupils
Note: Tie in two strands of black chenille and wrap the white chenille
        forward. Tie in the wing with the barbs stripped from the
        bottom. Pull the black chenille forward, one strand on each side
        to support the wing and bind at the head. Tie down the wing at
        the rear and clip the tip of the wing to form a tail as pictured.

The Bristleback was developed specifically for crappie fishing by veteran
Florida panfish specialist, Tom Lentz, who describes it as a modification
of a West Coast saltwater pattern that he discovered some years ago.

Tied by Tom Lentz

BUCKTAIL MUDDLER (NATURAL)

Hook: Straight eye, wide gape for bass; 3X or 4X long for panfish
Body: Braided pearl Polyflash wrapped over the rear ⅔ of the shank
Wing: Natural brown bucktail over which is pearl crystal flash and
        black bucktail followed by peacock herl
Head and collar: Natural deer body hair spun and clipped short and flat
        at the bottom; flat on the sides leaving a short deer hair collar
Eyes: Solid plastic, set high on the head

The Bucktail Muddler was developed by John Gierach of Longmont,
Colorado, for bass or panfish. It may be tied in natural or dyed colors and
fished on the surface as a slider or below the surface using a split shot or
sinking line.

Tied by John Gierach

Tied by Tom Nixon

BUG EYE INTEGRATION

Hook: Down eye, 4X long
Underbody: Yarn, built up
Body: Silver braided Mylar tubing
Tail: Unravelled strands of tubing
Wing: Brown bucktail on top and white bucktail on the bottom, tied on with the tips facing forward
Head: Brown bucktail pulled back over the top and the white bucktail pulled back underneath the hook, together forming the bullet head and completing the wing
Eyes: Solid plastic set into the head which must be heavily cemented before and after the eyes have been applied

In writing about this fly, Tom Nixon states that Bug Eye Integration is "a fantastic piece of bass-harvesting machinery (that) has done its thing on smallmouth and spotted Kentucky bass, as well as large-mouth and white bass."

Tied by Tom Nixon

CALCASIEU PIG BOAT

Hook: Straight eye, heavy wire
Body: Black chenille, heavy
Body hackle: Black, tied in by the butt and palmered
Collar: About 60 strands of black rubber hackle evenly distributed
Head: Black, with a yellow eye and red pupil

Inspired by the Arbogast Hawaiian Wiggler lure, Tom Nixon tied the first Pig Boat about 1950 and introduced it on Louisiana's Calcasieu River. This is the original all-black dressing, but it may be tied in other colors as well.

Tied by Farrow Allen

CARDINELLE

Hook: Down eye, 4X to 6X long
Body: Fluorescent red yarn
Wing: Fluorescent red Fishair over which is cerise marabou
Collar: Yellow hackle
Head: Fluorescent red or orange

Originated by Paul Kukonen of Worcester, Massachusetts, the Cardinelle has been successful on just about anything that swims, including bass and panfish. Due to its high visibility it is especially valuable in cloudy or off-colored water.

CLOUSER CRIPPLED MINNOW

Hook: Down eye, 3X or 4X long
Tail: Sparse yellow marabou over which are a few strands of pearlescent crystal flash and white marabou
Body: White yarn
Throat: Red yarn
Shellback: Peacock herl pulled over
Skirt and collar: Rusty-orange deer body hair on the top half only
Head: Natural white deer body hair, spun and trimmed into the shape of a diving head

Bob Clouser, a smallmouth guide and fly-shop owner from Middletown, Pennsylvania, designed the Crippled Minnow to be cast onto large slicks in smallmouth rivers, or into quiet shoreline cover where bass hang out waiting for a meal to appear. At rest the marabou tail dangles invitingly just below the surface, and shivers and squirms when twitched.

Tied by Bob Clouser

CLOUSER DEEP MINNOW (PERCH)

Hook: Down eye, 3X or 4X long
Eyes: Lead dumbbell eyes, painted red with black pupils and secured with olive thread
Throat: Yellow bucktail
Wing: Gold Flashabou and gold crystal flash over which is olive bucktail
Note: The orientation of Clouser Minnows is with the hook point up.

The Clouser Deep Minnows were developed for getting to bottom-hugging smallmouth lying in deep water. Lefty Kreh was so impressed with Clouser's Deep Minnow that he once wrote that it was "the best streamer I have ever used." Many others apparently agree because the popularity of this fly has skyrocketed.

Tied by Bob Clouser

CLOUSER DEEP MINNOW (ULTRA)

Hook: Down eye, 3X or 4X long, heavy wire
Eyes: Lead dumbbell eyes, painted red with black pupils, secured with gray thread
Throat: Polar bear Ultra Hair
Wing: Light blue Ultra Hair over which is pearlescent and silver crystal flash over which is smoke Ultra Hair
Note: Orientation of the fly dressing is with the hook point up.

The early Clouser Deep Minnows were dressed with natural and dyed bucktail. With the introduction of Ultra Hair, Clouser says that his fly achieves ". . . the transluscent effect . . . given off by most baitfish during movement." Also, he says they (Ultra Hair designs) are "very effective when used during clear water conditions." Color combinations vary to match natural baitfish, or as you chose.

Tied by Bob Clouser

Tied by Bud Priddy

CRIPPLED PERCH

Hook: Straight eye, wide gape. The orientation of the dressing is with the hook rotated 90° and the point facing directly away

Tail: Two yellow hackles and two pairs of olive dyed grizzly hackles curving out; gray ghost crystal flash on top and orange on the bottom

Pectoral Fins: Short white hackle tips

Marabou skirt: Olive over orange

Deer hair skirt: Olive over orange

Diving collar and head: Olive deer body hair stacked over orange red and yellow as shown and trimmed in the shape of a diver (oriented to the "true" bend of the hook)

Eyes: Solid plastic

This fly, designed by Bud Priddy of San Antonio, Texas, fishes on its side and imitates a crippled perch struggling to dive beneath the surface.

Tied by Larry Dahlberg

DAHLBERG FLASHDANCER

Hook: Straight eye, standard wire

Tail: Red marabou

Body: White chenille

Wing: Gold Flashabou

Head and collar: Natural deer body hair, spun and trimmed flat and clean on the bottom as shown

Larry Dahlberg designed this fly as a teenager ". . . for the old ladies and little kids to use at the fly-fishing-only smallmouth camp where I guided." During those years of guiding it proved to be more productive "than all the rest of the flies combined." It is the turbulence that's created by the clipped-deer-hair head that activates the limp Flashabou. "I've used this pattern with stiffer tinsels . . . and it simply isn't anywhere near as effective" Dahlberg states.

Tied by Larry Dahlberg

DAHLBERG FLOATING MINNOW

Hook: Straight eye, 6X to 8X long

Tail: Rusty red marabou

Underbody: Stainless steel or aluminum tape folded over closed-cell foam that has been glued to the top of the hook and colored black with a marking pen

Body: Braided silver Mylar tubing, painted to imitate a minnow and coated with 5-minute epoxy

Eyes: Hollow plastic

Note: Dahlberg says to keep the hook as flush to the belly as possible, this creates a more stable fly and the widest possible hook gape.

Inspired by Hal Jansen's minnow designs, Dahlberg developed the Floating Minnow for float tubing in Lake Michigan and fishing to large cruising brown trout. It is notably effective on surface-feeding bass in extremely clear water, as well as subsurface bass when fished on a high-density sinking line.

DEBBIE'S SUNNY

Hook: Straight eye, wide gape, with the shank bent towards you in the horizontal plane in a wide, even curve

Tail: Four olive hen hackle tips, one pair angling up and the other pair down to give the impression of a forked tail, cemented at the base

Body: Olive deer body hair stacked over very pale yellow and white deer body hair, (denser towards the center). Trim flat and "saucer-shaped," following the bend previously made in the hook shank, and add details with waterproof marking pens

Fins: Paired olive hen hackle tips, set into the deer hair and glued with Goop, after the body has been trimmed

Eyes: Solid plastic

Note: The body may be coated with clear silicone rubber for a more durable fly or tied flat in a horizontal plane.

When the hook is properly bent, Debbie's Sunny is a good imitation of an injured baby sunfish, struggling at the surface.

Tied by Tom Farmer

DICK'S DOWN EAST SMELT

Hook: Straight eye, silver

Tail: Two pale blue dun saddle hackles

Body: White sheep fleece, and a length of pearl Estaz chenille. The Estaz chenille is tied to the hook shank at the rear. A dubbing loop is formed with thread and the Estaz is twisted together with short bunches of white sheep fleece. The resulting dubbing is wrapped around the shank and trimmed to shape

Eyes: Solid plastic

Note: The top of the body is colored with gray and olive waterproof marking pens.

"Down East" in Maine there are numerous lakes and ponds which contain large populations of both smallmouth bass and rainbow smelt. Each spring the smelt gather at the mouths of rivers and streams and the bass follow. A good smelt imitation will catch bass under these conditions and this pattern is easy to cast and very durable.

Tied by Dick Stewart

E. S. MINNOW (SHAD)

Hook: Straight eye, 3X long, inverted in vise

Underbody: Tapered lead tape, folded over the shank

Tail: White marabou

Body: The balance of the white marabou tail is twisted into a chenille-like rope and wrapped over the minnow-shaped underbody

Rib: Oval silver tinsel

Wing: Pearl crystal flash over which is gray marabou

Gills: Red crystal flash

Collar: Gray over white deer body hair

Head: Gray stacked over white deer body hair, trimmed flat as shown

Eyes: Yellow and black lacquer, coated with epoxy

The E.S. Minnow was originated by Eric Schmuecker for fishing southern impoundments with populations of shad minnows. As a professional tier, Schmuecker has been involved with Bass Pro Shops as well as his father's company, Wapsi Fly, and he markets Perch and Shiner E.S. Minnows as well.

Tied by Eric Schmuecker

Tied by McKenzie Flies

FOAMIN' PERCH

Hook:	Straight eye
Body:	Oval gold tinsel
Wing:	Yellow marabou over which is a single dark olive marabou plume and dyed yellow grizzly hackles on each side with strands of pearlescent yellow crystal flash on the outside
Gills:	Bright red hackle applied as a collar
Head:	A circular piece cut from a sheet of yellow closed-cell foam (Ethafoam) trimmed and tied flat on top of the hook shank, curving down over the collar, and painted olive on top between the eyes
Eyes:	Solid plastic

This is one of a series of Foamin' Bass Bugs that was developed by Bill Galloway. The technique is simple and easily lends itself to tying shad, shiners, frogs, etc.

FUZZABOU SHAD

Hook:	Straight eye, heavy wire
Tail:	Four to six white marabou plumes with the stems removed with silver crystal flash on top and grizzly hackles on the side
Skirt:	Soft grizzly hackle
Eyes:	Lead, painted white with black pupils
Head:	Gray lamb's wool, spun and trimmed to shape

This is one of a series of marabou-minnow imitations developed by Jimmy Nix. Unlike Nix's Shinabou patterns (which see) the Fuzzabous all feature wool heads and lead eyes.

Tied by Umpqua Feather Merchants

GRAY GHOST

Hook:	Down eye, 6X long
Butt:	Flat silver tinsel
Body:	Golden-yellow floss
Rib:	Flat silver tinsel
Wing:	Peacock herl over which are several golden pheasant crests and two pairs of gray hackles
Throat:	Pearlescent crystal flash (optional) and white bucktail over which is a short golden pheasant crest, curving upwards
Cheeks:	Silver pheasant body feather and jungle cock eye (optional)

A classic Maine streamer originated by Carrie Stevens for landlocked-salmon fishing. This variation is one that George Kesel of Hunter's Fly Shop in New Boston, New Hampshire, ties for smallmouth fishing in New England lakes that contain large smelt populations.

Tied by George Kesel

HORNBERG SPECIAL

Hook: Down eye, 3X or 4X long
Body: Flat silver tinsel
Underwing: Two short yellow hackle tips or yellow calftail
Wing: A pair of matched gray mallard flank or well-marked mallard breast feathers
Cheeks: Jungle cock or substitute
Collar: Soft grizzly hackle
Note: Teal, woodduck and pintail wings are common variations

Although the Hornberg Special originated in the midwest where it was first marketed by the Weber Tackle Company in Wisconsin, its biggest fans are in the northeast where Hornbergs are fished both wet and dry in a variety of colors. Tied in small sizes it's very appealing to most panfish, and in large sizes it's deadly on bass, but not commonly used.

Tied by Farrow Allen

HORNBERG STREAMER

Hook: Down eye, 4X long
Body: Flat silver tinsel
Wing: Sparse yellow bucktail flanked by broad webby grizzly hackles
Cheeks: Mallard flank and barred woodduck
Collar: Soft grizzly hackle

This streamer variation of the popular Hornberg Special (which see) was introduced by Dick Stewart and Bob Leeman in their book *Trolling Flies for Trout and Salmon.* Though originated for trout and landlocked salmon, it is used on lakes with mixed species where it works best on bass.

Tied by Dick Stewart

KEEL BUG (YELLOW/BLACK)

Hook: Keel Fly
Tail: Two black over two yellow hackles, veiled by yellow bucktail, about half as long as the hackles
Body: The butt ends of the yellow bucktail used for the tail, evenly distributed around the hook shank and secured with criss-cross wraps of black thread
Hackle: Black, heavy
Wing: Yellow bucktail
Head: Yellow deer body hair, spun and clipped in a round shape
Note: A single strip of heavy lead wire can be bound to the bottom of the hook for weight and to help keep the hook point up.

Tom Nixon tied this nearly-weedless streamer after having been sent a sample of the first Keel Fly hooks. The design of the hook allows the fly to swim hook point up and the heavily-dressed hair wing protects the point from fouling.

Tied by Tom Nixon

Baitfish

Tied by Tom Schmuecker

LEAD EYED BUNNY BOOGER

Hook:	Straight eye, short shank
Eyes:	Lead, painted yellow with black pupils
Tail:	Tapered rabbit fur strip, dyed chartreuse, skin side facing up
Body:	Chartreuse cross-cut rabbit strip, wrapped around the hook shank and in front of the eyes
Head:	Red
Note:	Chartreuse, white, black and olive seem to be the best colors.

Tom Schmuecker of Wapsi Fly, Inc., in Mountain Home, Arkansas, developed this fly over a period of time and in so doing he originated "Lead eyes." His first Bunny Booger was tied with plastic eyes and lead wire. The next version used bead-chain eyes, and this was followed by bead-chain eyes filled with lead. Later Schmuecker built a mold to cast solid lead balls that were connected by wire and eventually he developed the dumbbell-shaped lead eyes used today.

Tied by Lefty Kreh

LEFTY'S RED & WHITE

Hook:	Straight eye, heavy wire, silver
Tail:	A few strands of pearl crystal flash and six white hackles, curving out
Body:	Two red hackles and a center white hackle, (or vice-versa) wound over a base of red thread
Eyes:	Lead (optional)

Lefty's Red & White was originated by angler and author Lefty Kreh. At one time he considered it the "single most effective underwater fly that I have ever used for bass." Any fly that carries this endorsement from such an experienced angler should not be overlooked.

Tied by Dick Stewart

LI'L PICKEREL

Hook:	3X long, gold
Wing:	Olive bucktail, over which is a small amount of olive marabou, flanked by several grizzly hackles dyed olive
Eyes:	Hollow plastic
Collar:	Soft grizzly, dyed olive
Head:	Long and tapered from olive tying thread that is coated with epoxy

The Li'l Pickerel was designed by Dick Stewart and introduced in his 1989 book, *Bass Flies*. It is tied in a style that is reminiscent of certain saltwater flies, and lends itself well to imitating the long narrow profile of an immature pickerel. The long "nose" keeps bigger pickerel teeth away from the leader and the hollow eyes help to keep the fly suspended close to the surface.

Bass & Panfish
40

LLAMA

Hook: Down eye, 3X or 4X long
Tail: Soft grizzly hackle barbs
Body: Red floss or wool
Rib: Oval gold tinsel
Wing: Woodchuck body hair including guard hairs and underfur
Collar: Soft grizzly hackle, tied back
Note: It is very important to include all the underfur when tying in the woodchuck wing; it is this that seems to give life to this fly.

Eric Leiser has been a pioneer in the use of groundhog (woodchuck) fur in fly tying, and he popularized the Llama in the 1970s. When properly tied this fly has a very lifelike appearance in the water, and fish often find it irresistible. We sometimes tie the Llama with different body colors.

Tied by Dick Stewart

LOPEZ MINNOW

Hook: Down eye, 3X or 4X long
Tail: Fluorescent green marabou
Underbody: Lead wire
Body: Yellow glow-in-the-dark (Everglow) tubing
Throat: Fluorescent green marabou
Wing: Yellow bucktail, over which is green bucktail, over which is peacock herl, bound at the rear with fluorescent green thread
Head: Fluorescent green, with a painted white eye and black pupil
Note: It is very important to even up the the tips of the bucktail used for the wing.

Tom Lentz submitted this pattern which he says works well when bass are chasing baitfish. The Lopez Minnow may be tied in a variety of colors, and should be ". . . retrieved as fast as possible." The basic design was borrowed from west coast saltwater fly tiers.

Tied by Tom Lentz

LOUISIANA MICKEY FINN

Hook: Down eye or straight eye, 4X to 6X long
Tail: A short section of black and white barred woodduck
Butt: Orange chenille
Body: Silver tinsel chenille ribbed with gold tinsel chenille
Wing: Yellow over which is red over which is yellow bucktail or calftail
Cheek: Barred black and white woodduck
Head: Black with a yellow eye and red pupil

This is Tom Nixon's bass fly modification of the Mickey Finn (which see), a streamer with its origins in the coldwater lakes and rivers of eastern Canada and New England. From Nixon's observations "bass want something with body and bulk, something worth opening their mouth for," and the Louisiana Mickey Finn clearly meets these requirements.

Tied by Tom Nixon

Tied by Umpqua Feather Merchants

MARABOU MUDDLER (WHITE)

Hook:	Down eye, 3X or 4X long
Tail:	Red hackle barbs
Body:	Oval silver tinsel or silver tinsel chenille
Wing:	White marabou tied full, over which are several strands of peacock herl
Head:	Natural deer body hair spun and clipped to form a head and collar
Note:	Marabou muddlers are often tied with an underbody of lead wire to counter the tendency of clipped deer hair to float. Other popular colors are black, yellow and olive or a combination of these. (see Whitlock's Multi-colored Marabou Muddler)

This variation of the standard Muddler Minnow (which see) was developed and is generally credited to the innovative mind of Dan Bailey. It is often tied in very large sizes with wings as large as marabou plumes will permit. In large sizes it's a good pattern for off-color water.

Tied by Farrow Allen

MARABOU STREAMER (YELLOW)

Hook:	Down eye, 4X long
Body:	Gold Mylar tubing secured with red thread
Wing:	Two golden pheasant crests tied flat over which is yellow marabou and strands of peacock herl

This simple marabou streamer was tied for fishing the lower reaches of Lake Champlain's tributaries, many of which are heavily populated with smallmouth bass. Beginning in late April, smallmouth bass in New England move out of lakes and into tributaries to spawn. During these periods smallmouth can be taken with a marabou streamer fished slowly.

Tied by Umpqua Feather Merchants

MATUKA (OLIVE)

Hook:	Down eye, 4X long
Body:	Olive chenille or yarn with a turn or two of red wool at the throat
Rib:	Oval gold tinsel
Wing:	Several badger or grizzly hackles dyed olive, secured to the body by wraps of oval tinsel
Collar:	Badger or grizzly hackle dyed olive

By most accounts, the Matuka style of securing a feather wing was developed in New Zealand and appeared in this country during the late 1960s. It gained acceptance in the mid 1970s through the enthusiasm of tiers like Harry Darbee, Doug Swisher and Dave Whitlock. The particular orientation of the Matuka wing makes it almost foul-proof.

McNALLY MAGNUM

Hook: Straight eye, stainless steel
Body: Yellow chenille
Wing: Six or more yellow hackles, long and wide
Collar: Red hackle
Head: Red

A big, bright streamer pattern that was designed in the 1950s by Tom McNally specifically for northern pike, it became readily apparent to McNally that big bass were (and still are) attracted to this fly.

Tied by Farrow Allen

MICKEY FINN

Hook: Down eye, 4X to 6X long
Body: Flat silver tinsel ribbed with oval silver tinsel, or silver Mylar tubing secured in back with red tying thread
Wing: A small bunch of yellow bucktail or calftail over which is an equal amount of red over which is a larger bunch of yellow hair, equal in size to the first two bunches combined

The Mickey Finn was popularized during the 1930s by John Alden Knight, the author of the Solunar Tables that chart the phases of the moon and their relationship to times when fish feed. The Mickey Finn is easy to tie and the colors are unmistakably effective on bass and panfish.

Tied by Farrow Allen

MIRACLE PERCH

Rear section - Hook: Straight eye, wide gape
Tail: Four olive dyed hen hackle tips, one pair angling up and the other down
Body: Olive deer body hair stacked over white and pale yellow deer body hair and trimmed to shape
Front section - Hook: Straight eye, wide gape, one size larger than the rear hook
Note: At this point tie in a piece of 12 lb. stainless wire and connect the completed rear section to the front hook with a wire loop.
Body: Olive deer body hair stacked over white and pale yellow deer body hair and trimmed to shape
Eyes: Solid plastic
Note: After both body sections have been trimmed to your satisfaction, details and highlights are applied with orange, red and dark olive waterproof marking pens.

Tom Farmer tied this yellow perch variation of Tim England's original design, the Miracle Minnow.

Tied by Tom Farmer

Baitfish

Tied by Dick Stewart

MIZZOLIAN (MISSOULIAN) SPOOK

Hook:	Down eye, 4X long
Tail:	Very light speckled turkey wing quill sections
Butt:	Red chenille
Body:	White yarn
Rib:	Flat gold tinsel
Wing:	Barred teal flank over which are very light speckled turkey wing quill segments
Collar:	Natural gray deer body hair on top and white on the bottom
Head:	White deer body hair, spun and trimmed as shown and cemented

This predominately white variation of the Muddler Minnow developed as a trout fly around Three Forks, Montana, on the Missouri River. Its popularity is due in part to the enthusiasm of Dan Bailey's Fly Fishing Shop in Livingston, Montana, where it was recognized as a big fish taker. In large sizes it is very effective on bass.

Tied by George Kesel

MUDDLER MINNOW

Hook:	Down eye, 3X or 4X long
Tail:	Mottled turkey wing quill sections
Body:	Flat gold tinsel
Wing:	Gray squirrel tail and sparse pearlescent crystal flash (optional) over which are matched sections of mottled turkey wing quill
Head and collar:	Natural deer body hair, spun and clipped as shown

The first Muddler Minnow was tied by Don Gapen of Minnesota. It was designed to imitate a sculpin for use in brook-trout fishing in northern Ontario. If tied with a large deer-hair head, the Muddler can be greased and fished on the surface as a bass bug or a wounded minnow. Tied with a lead underbody and small deer-hair head, or a wool head, the Muddler can be fished deep.

Tied by Yvon Gendron

NEPTUNE STREAMER

Hook:	Down eye, 2X or 3X long
Body:	Flat silver (or gold) tinsel, wrapped half way up the body
Wing:	Broad silver badger (or golden badger) saddle hackles
Collar:	Badger hackle that matches the wing, wound heavily over the front half of the hook

Developed in 1962 by Yvon Gendron of Neptune Flies, in Drummondville, Quebec, the Neptune is his most effective bass streamer. It has accounted for many catches throughout Quebec and northern New England.

OZARK WEEDLESS BUCKTAIL

Hook: Straight eye, wet fly
Body: This fly consists entirely of six to eight distinct segments of hair, usually bucktail or skunk hair, in a combination of natural or dyed colors of your choice. Beginning at the rear of the hook shank each segment is tied on the underside of the hook shank with the tips pointing toward the rear. The butt ends are then brought upright, half on each side of the hook shank, folded toward the back, and secured on top of the hook shank with thread wraps which proceed from right to left. The segment is completed by a final layer of thread wraps from left to right.

Originating many years ago in the upper midwest this fly has been known, in its variations, by several names including Miss Westwood's Bass Bug and Mississippi Bass Bug.

Tied by Dick Stewart

PIC-A-BUGGER

Hook: Straight eye, heavy wire
Tail: Two plumes of fluorescent green marabou with chartreuse crystal flash in between
Body: Fluorescent green chenille
Hackle: Fluorescent green, tied in by the tip and palmered forward
Collar: Chartreuse hackle
Head: Fluorescent green thread with a band of red thread at the rear

The Pic-A-Bugger was originally tied for saltwater striped bass in Long Island Sound by Tom Piccolo, of the Sportsman's Den in Cos Cob, Connecticut. It has since proved to be an effective subsurface pattern for largemouth bass.

Tied by Tom Piccolo

POP LIPS PERCH

Hook: Straight eye, wide gape
Wing: Orange crystal flash, short orange bucktail, longer yellow bucktail and two yellow dyed grizzly hackles outside
Skirt: A collar of dyed yellow grizzly hackle with orange crystal flash and orange lamb's wool, on the bottom only
Wool head: Tan and olive lamb's wool stacked over yellow lamb's wool trimmed to shape leaving a "bib" of wool to build the diving lip
Head and lip: Clear silicone rubber is spread over the wool head, shaped as shown and sprinkled with sparkle-glitter flakes.
Eyes: Peel-off, stick-on Lure Eyes
Note: After applying the eyes and glitter flakes, add a final coat of silicone rubber.

This and the following Pop Lip flies all wobble and dart when retrieved underwater. Bob Popovics has cleverly devised a method of making flies behave like many lures and plugs.

Tied by Bob Popovics

Baitfish

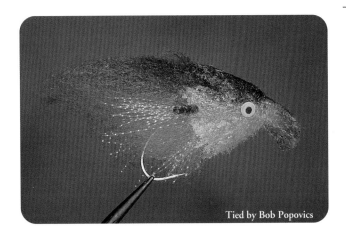

Tied by Bob Popovics

POP LIPS PUMPKINSEED

Hook: Straight eye, wide gape
Wing: Green lamb's wool over orange lamb's wool, with an orange crystal flash on the sides and bottom. A spot is drawn on each side behind the head with a black marking pen
Wool head: The head is a continuation of wing, trimmed to shape leaving a "bib" of wool to build the diving lip
Head and lip: Clear silicone rubber spread over the wool, and shaped as shown (to form the lip work the silicone into the bib, shape with your fingers and trim to shape when partially cured)
Eyes: Peel-off, stick-on Lure Eyes
Note: Dow Chemical's "Dap", Devcon's "Clear Silicone Rubber" and G.E.'s "Silicone II" are a few of the brand-name silicones that have been used by the originator with success.

This is Bob Popovics' version of one of a big bass' favorite snacks. The body is flattened like a sunfish.

Tied by Bob Popovics

POP LIPS SHINER

Hook: Straight eye, wide gape
Body: Tinsel chenille
Throat: Silver crystal flash
Head and wing: Light gray lamb's wool, tied in front of the body with the long strands representing the minnow body and the head trimmed to shape leaving a "bib" of wool to build the diving lip
Head and lip: Clear silicone rubber spread over the wool, shaped as shown, and sprinkled with sparkle-glitter flakes
Eyes: Peel-off stick-on Lure Eyes
Note: After applying the eyes and glitter flakes add a final coat silicone rubber to the head and lip.

Bob Popovics' Pop-Lips flies swim and wiggle when retrieved. Popovics is an innovative fly tier from Seaside Park, New Jersey, who has developed most of his flies for saltwater fishing. The three imitations shown here represent a long-awaited departure into freshwater flies.

Tied by Doug Tucker-Eccher

RATTLIN' BLUEGILL

Hook: Straight eye, 4X long, tied hook point up
Tail: Strands of black ostrich herl
Underbody: A glass rattle chamber secured to the hook and dubbed over with yellow sparkle dubbing
Body: Blue Flashabou Minnow Body, tied down in back, with the rear portion unravelled over the ostrich tail
Throat: Unravelled butts of blue Flashabou Minnow Body, pulled down and fanned out
Gills: Scarlet hackle
Wing: Olive rabbit fur strip
Head: Olive, orange and yellow lamb's wool stacked over white lamb's wool and trimmed as shown (Some of the olive wool from the head should be left long and pulled over the rabbit fur strip)
Eyes: Optional

Doug Tucker-Eccher who designed this fly suggests using this pattern as a guide for creating any minnow you like.

RED & WHITE BUCKTAIL

Hook: Down eye, 4X to 6X long
Body: Flat silver tinsel or silver Mylar tubing secured at the rear with red thread
Rib: Oval silver tinsel (omitted if Mylar tubing is used)
Wing: White bucktail over which is red bucktail followed by white bucktail or peacock herl

As evidenced by the universal popularity of the Eppinger Dardevle, the combination of red and white in a lure are hard to beat when it comes to bass fishing. For a simple and highly effective bucktail streamer, this pattern can be tied in a full range of sizes for both bass and panfish.

Tied by Farrow Allen

SHENK'S SCULPIN (BLACK)

Hook: Straight eye, 2X or 3X long
Tail: Black marabou, slightly longer than the hook shank
Body: Black fur applied heavily over the rear ⅔ of the hook shank using a dubbing loop and trimmed flat on the bottom, tapering larger toward the head
Head: Spun black deer body hair, trimmed broad and flat like the head of a natural sculpin
Pectoral fins: Untrimmed black deer body hair

Ed Shenk's sculpin imitation was developed in the early 1960s for trout on Pennsylvania's Letort Spring Run. Over the years it has accounted for many eastern smallmouth in rivers that contain sizable populations of sculpins.

Tied by Ed Shenk

SHENK'S WHITE STREAMER

Hook: Straight eye, 3X or 4X long
Tail: White marabou , slightly longer than the hook shank
Body: White or cream fox fur applied heavily with a dubbing loop, and trimmed flat along the sides like a shad minnow
Head: Gray or black thread built up
Eyes: Painted white eye and black pupil (optional)

This unorthodox soft-bodied streamer was developed in 1962 by Ed Shenk of Carlisle, Pennsylvania. Like his Sculpin, the White Streamer was tied originally as a trout fly and later proved its value on bass.

Tied by Ed Shenk

Baitfish

Tied by Jimmy Nix

SHINEABOU SHAD

Hook: Straight eye, heavy wire, silver
Body: Silver gray Antron over the rear ⅔ of the hook
Skirt: Fluorescent gray marabou veiling the body with pearl and silver or gold crystal flash on each side and peacock herl over the top
Gills: Red fluff from the base of a hackle
Sides: A pair of natural gray mallard breast or flank feathers on each side, slightly shorter than the marabou
Head: Dyed pearl gray deer body hair, spun and clipped as shown
Eyes: Solid plastic

Along the Gulf Coast from Texas to Florida and as far north as Tennessee, Arkansas and Oklahoma schools of threadfin and gizzard shad comprise a major part of a bass' diet. According to Jimmy Nix, who designed the Shineabou Shad to imitate these prolific forage fish, his inspiration came from the Hornberg Special and a Dave Whitlock marabou shad pattern.

Tied by Jimmy Nix

SHINEABOU SHAD (WOOL HEAD)

Dressing: Same as for the Shineabou Shad above except for the eyes and head
Eyes: Lead "dumbbell" eyes painted yellow with black pupils
Head: Dyed gray lamb's wool, spun and trimmed around the lead eyes as shown

Replacing the customary deer-hair head with wool results in better water absorption, so the fly sinks more rapidly. Swapping lead eyes for the plastic eyes adds to the increased sink rate of these designs.

Tied by Jimmy Nix

SHINEABOU SHINER

Hook: Straight eye, wide gape
Tail: White bucktail and 6 to 8 silver gray hackles over which is silver, gold and pearl crystal flash or Flashabou
Body: Silver gray Antron, dubbed half way up the hook shank
Skirt: Silver gray marabou fibers, stripped from the stem and spun around the hook shank to veil the Antron body
Throat: Two bunches of fluff from the base of a dyed red hackle, one on each side
Overwing: Pearl and silver crystal flash or Flashabou over which is peacock herl or peacock crystal flash
Collar: Gray deer body hair
Head and collar: Gray deer body hair, spun and clipped to shape
Eyes: Solid plastic

SHINEABOU SHINER (WOOL HEAD)

Dressing: Same as for the Shineabou Shiner above except for the eyes and
head
Eyes: Lead "dumbbells" painted yellow with black pupils
Head: Dyed gray lamb's wool, spun and trimmed around the lead eyes
as shown

For catching really big bass, it's hard to beat a live shiner. Jimmy Nix's
Shineabou Shiner is one of the best imitations around and about as close
as you can get to a live shiner without actually sticking your hand into the
live-bait well. Both variations are designed for subsurface fishing, but the
deer-hair Shiner runs shallow while the lead-eyed one runs deep, depending on the size of lead eyes you use. Nix says that the Shineabou Shiner is
"one of my best big-fish flies."

Tied by Jimmy Nix

SHINEBOU SUNFISH

Hook: Straight eye, wide gape
Body: Olive Antron
Rib: Copper wire
Wing: Four broad grizzly hen hackles dyed olive and applied matuka
style, two on top and two secured underneath
Skirt: Sparse olive marabou
Gills: Two bunches of fluff from the base of a dyed red hackle
Collar: Olive deer body hair over orange deer body hair
Head: Olive with stripes black deer body hair stacked over orange deer
body hair at the throat and all olive at the head, trimmed flat and
sunfish-like
Eyes: Solid plastic

Immature sunfish are always available to bass, and this is a good looking
imitation. It is one of the newer additions to Jimmy Nix's Shineabou series
of bass minnows.

Tied by Jimmy Nix

SHINEABOU SUNFISH (WOOL HEAD)

Dressing: Same as for the Shineabou Shad above except for the eyes and
head
Eyes: Lead "dumbbells" painted yellow with black pupils
Head: Olive and black lamb's wool over an orange lamb's wool
throat, and all olive at the head, trimmed flat on the sides as
shown

Tied by Jimmy Nix

Tied by Tom Nixon

SOWELA

Hook: Straight eye, 4X long
Body: Yellow chenille, heavy
Hackle: Grizzly, palmered over the body
Wing: Six long grizzly hackles, splayed outward
Eyes: Glass taxidermy, clear with black pupils, or silver bead chain
Head: Black

Tom Nixon gives credit for this streamer to a "Cajun friend" from Louisiana and describes it as having ". . . size, bulk, action and enough weight to put it at any harvesting depth desired." It is best when allowed to sink several feet below the surface and retrieved so the grizzly wings open and close in a ". . . gentle undulating, seductive action."

Tied by Dick Stewart

SPUDDLER

Hook: Down eye, 3X or 4X long
Tail: Brown calftail
Body: Creamy yellow mohair yarn, dubbing or similar material
Throat: Red yarn
Wing: Brown calftail over which are broad webby grizzly hackles dyed brown with a short bunch of red squirrel tail on each side
Head and Collar: Brown deer body hair, spun and trimmed fairly flat as shown, the collar is over upper half of the fly
Note: Frequently this and other deer hair sculpin imitations are heavily weighted with an underbody of lead wire to get them to the river bottom where sculpins live.

Popularized by Dan Bailey's Fly Shop in Livingston, Montana, where it was developed by Bailey, Red Monical and Don Williams. In rivers where sculpins are abundant, the Spuddler is a killing pattern on bass in spite of its Western trout heritage.

Tied by Jim Stewart

STEWART'S CHUB DARTER (BLUE/BLACK)

Hook: Straight eye, wide gape
Tail: A pair of pale gray hackles outside of which are light and dark blue dyed grizzly hackles curving out; over is blue flashabou and silver crystal flash
Butt: Fluorescent rose chenille
Skirt: Natural gray deer body hair on the sides and blue over black in the center
Body: Gray, blue and black deer body hair stacked over white, ending with an all white head and trimmed as shown and cemented in front and on the bottom
Eyes: Hollow plastic

When retrieved with short quick strips, Jim Stewart's Chub Darter darts from side to side or it can be made to dive below the surface. In this, and other Jim Stewart flies, the influence that bass casting plugs have had on his fly designs can be seen.

STEWART'S DYING SIDEWINDER SHINER

Note: This fly is tied so the body rests flat upon the water
Hook: Straight eye, wide gape
Tail: Short light orange marabou over which are 4 white schlappen hackles curving down and two shorter grizzly hackles
Skirt: Natural over which is white deer body hair
Body: Natural gray stripes of deer body hair stacked over white deer body hair including an orange throat and white head, trimmed as shown, flat on the underside with a 45 degree angle "cut" at the throat position. The front and the underside are cemented
Eyes: Solid plastic
Spots: Solid black plastic beads

The Dying Sidewinder Shiner was designed by Jim Stewart to float on its side, hook point down. When retrieved the angled throat causes the fly to appear as if it were a minnow struggling to swim upright.

Tied by Jim Stewart

TÊTE DE BOULE (ORANGE)

Hook: Straight eye, 6X long
Wing: Yellow and light orange polar bear substitute over which is pearl Flashabou and golden yellow polar bear substitute topped by four long hot orange hackles
Head: Fluorescent orange chenille
Eyes: Hollow plastic, with single strands of fluorescent red chenille pulled forward from behind the body to imitate eyebrows

Jacques Juneau is well-known in Quebec as a fly tier and graphic artist. This unique looking streamer typifies the style of many large Quebec flies that are primarily fished for big northern pike. The Tête de Boule is tied at the rear of a long shank hook to protect the leader from the pike's sharp teeth. This fly has also accounted for many large bass in lakes throughout Quebec and Ontario.

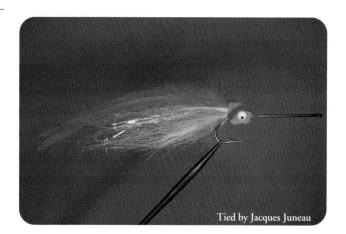

Tied by Jacques Juneau

THIEF

Hook: 3X or 4X long
Tail: Red wing quill section
Body: Flat silver tinsel
Rib: Oval silver tinsel
Wing: Gray squirrel tail outside of which are wide dark mottled turkey wing quill sections
Head: Black chenille

The Thief is a dark variation of the Muddler Minnow that Dan Gapen developed for bass and crappie fishing in northern Minnesota. Dan is the son of Don Gapen who originated the Muddler Minnow (which see). The Thief uses the proven Muddler profile, darkens the overall appearance and adds a chenille head that sinks more readily than deer hair. The pattern seems to work best in murky, discolored water.

Tied by David Lucca

Tied by Ian James

TIPPET WHISKER

Hook: Salmon, Bartleet, or down eye, 2X long
Body: Black chenille
Wing: Matched golden pheasant tippet feathers
Eyes: Silver bead chain
Note: Variations include substituting Amherst pheasant tippets for the wing or varying the color of the chenille body - chartreuse, white and purple are good choices.

Ian James of Balmoral Flies in Guelph, Ontario, tied the Tippet Whisker in 1986 as a variation of a British stillwater trout fly using large tippet feathers to offer a broad silhouette for bass in off-colored water. In spite of its odd appearance, James says the Tippet Whisker ". . . ranks next to leeches in its fish catching properties." This fly is reminiscent of some of the bass wet flies used in the late 1800s and early 1900s.

Tied by Thomas Wölfle

TOM'S BANDIT

Hook: Straight eye, 4X long
Underbody: Neutral colored Furry Foam or similar
Body: Pearlescent crystal chenille
Rib: Silver or gold wire
Wing: Two blue dyed webby grizzly hackles, secured to the body with the rib, Matuka style
Collar: Blue dyed grizzly
Eyes: Solid glass or plastic
Head: Large size light gray chenille, wound around the eyes and trimmed as shown

Originated by Thomas Wölfle of Munich, Germany, who uses this basic design to imitate a variety of different minnows. While Wölfle designed this for trout, we've found it to be a good basic minnow design for bass, too.

TROTH BULLHEAD

Hook: Salmon wet
Underbody: Lead wire (optional)
Tail: White bucktail over which is black marabou with strands of peacock herl on top
Body: White yarn
Shellback: The balance of black marabou and peacock herl used in the tail, pulled forward over the top of the body
Head and collar: Natural dark deer body hair, spun and clipped as shown. The top of the head may also be darkened with a black marking pen
Note: The original design uses black ostrich in place of the marabou and peacock herl.

Al Troth of Dillon, Montana, designed this fly in the early 1960s for trout fishing on the Madison River. For either trout or bass it is usually weighted and fished deep, close to the bottom.

Tied by George Kesel

WATERMAN'S SILVER OUTCAST

Hook: Straight eye, stainless steel or down eye, 3X long
Body: Flat silver tinsel
Wing: Sparse bunches of white over which is blue, and yellow bucktail or calftail topped by several strands peacock herl
Note: Waterman says that he usually adds a little silver Mylar (Flashabou) to the wing, and thinks it makes a more attractive fly.

Noted bass fisherman Charlie Waterman adapted this pattern to bass and saltwater fishing from a streamer he was given many years ago while fishing in the Florida Everglades. The man who gave him the fly called it a Silver Doctor. Waterman tried the fly in the Rockies and caught an unusually large trout while fishing with Dan Bailey. Bailey said it didn't look like any Silver Doctor he'd ever seen and renamed it "Waterman's Silver Outcast."

Tied by Farrow Allen

WEEDLESS WOOLY (YELLOW)

Hook: Straight eye, wide gape, tied point up
Underbody: Lead wire wrapped over the front ⅓ of the shank
Body: Yellow Furry Foam
Hackle: Two yellow, palmered over the body
Wing: Yellow bucktail over which is yellow marabou followed by pearl crystal flash and a large bunch of peacock herl over all
Head: Black thread, built up with a painted yellow eye and black pupil

The Weedless Wooly was designed to be "... an upside-down, largely weedless version of the good old Woolly Bugger" says its developer John Gierach of Longmont, Colorado. It's tied for bass or panfish in various colors including black, brown, olive and many of the same color combinations you might expect to see in standard Woolly Buggers (which see), and works well in heavy cover and submerged timber.

Tied by John Gierach

WHISTLER (RED & WHITE)

Hook: Straight eye, stainless steel
Wing: White bucktail outside of which are narrow bunches of red bucktail
Body: Red chenille, short
Collar: Soft white hackle, very heavy
Eyes: Silver bead chain, secured with red thread

This fly originated as part of a series of saltwater streamers that was created by Dan Blanton of San Jose, California. Blanton began tying the Whistlers in the mid 1960s, primarily for striped-bass fishing around San Francisco Bay. The red-and-white variation shown here is a favorite of many freshwater bass fishermen.

Tied by Doug Tucker-Eccher

Tied by Tom Nixon

WHITE TAIL GRIZZLY

Hook:	Straight eye, 2X long
Tail:	About 20 strands of white rubber hackle
Body:	Gray chenille
Hackle:	Soft grizzy saddle, palmered heavily
Head:	Black with yellow eyes and red pupils
Note:	As an option this fly may be weighted with lead wire or lead eyes.

In describing the White Tail Grizzly, Tom Nixon says that "...the gentle motion of the grizzly hackle fibers has a real come-hither appeal. The undulations of the white rubber tail definitely does things to a bass' basic reasoning processes." And if it is retrieved erratically, it should "...arouse the curiosity of all but the most mundane finny observers."

Tied by Dave Whitlock

WHITLOCK'S DEEP SHEEP CRAPPIE

Hook:	Long shank stainless steel, bent as shown and tied hook point up
Throat:	A ball of fluorescent red yarn or dubbing picked out, over this is pearlescent crystal flash and fine white (wool) streamer hair
Wing:	Pearlescent crystal flash over which is fine white and yellow (wool) streamer hair, over which is pearlescent yellow and pearl crystal flash and pale gray (wool) streamer hair topped by peacock crystal flash
Sides:	On each side: A strip of pearlescent Mylar trimmed to a point, outside of which is a single grizzly hackle
Cheeks:	Small mallard flank or breast feather
Eyes:	A flattened, chromed lead eye with a black pupil

Dave Whitlock's "sheep series" is a newly-developed style of baitfish imitation which results in flies that are more transparant and more suggestive than many earlier designs. This one sinks very quickly. See also the Whitlock Sheep Shad and Whitlock Sheep Sunfish.

Tied by Dave Whitlock

WHITLOCK'S HARE GRUB

Hook:	Down eye, wide gape
Legs:	Three pairs of gray and white rubber hackles with sparse silver crystal flash
Eyes:	Lead, painted white with red eyes and black pupils
Throat:	A long gray rabbit fur strip, skin side up, impaled over the hook point, brought forward under the hook and secured at the head
Wing:	A shorter gray rabbit fur strip, secured at the head and cemented to the rabbit strip below, virtually sandwiching the legs and hook shank between the upper and lower strips of fur

The Hare Grub and a companion fly, the Whitlock Hare Jig, are relatively new patterns from the innovative Dave Whitlock. Both are made possible by the availability of lead "dumbbell" eyes, and both feature the unique construction technique described above.

WHITLOCK'S MATCH-THE-MINNOW (PERCH)

Hook: Straight eye, 6X long, tied hook point up
Underbody: Aluminum, lead or Mylar tape, folded over the the hook shank and trimmed to a shape suggesting a minnow body
Body: Pearlescent gold Mylar tubing
Tail: A short bunch of soft orange fur or wool added when the Mylar tubing is secured at the rear
Wing: Two to four yellow dyed grizzly hackles, split around the hook point and glued along the entire top of the body
Throat: A short bunch of soft orange fur, wool and a stripe of red lacquer painted on the Mylar body suggesting the outline of the gills
Eyes: Solid plastic
Head: Gold lacquer

Dave Whitlock originated his Match-the-Minnow series for imitating just about every freshwater baitfish you can imagine. Additional details can be added by carefully painting the Mylar body.

Tied by Umpqua Feather Merchants

WHITLOCK'S MATUKA SCULPIN (TAN)

Hook: Straight eye, 3X long
Underbody: Lead wire (optional)
Body: Natural creamy-tan fur or yarn
Rib: Gold wire
Wing: Four ginger variant or cree hackles, tied in at the head and secured Matuka-style with the gold wire rib
Pectoral fins: Ringneck pheasant body feathers
Throat: Red yarn or dubbing
Collar: Top: Mixed clumps of black and dyed red-brown deer body hair
    Sides: Natural dark deer body hair
    Bottom: Cream colored deer body hair
Head: Alternating bands of black, red-brown, and natural gray deer body hair stacked over a mixture of cream, white and light natural gray deer body hair. The overall shape of the head should be trimmed broad and flat and rounded slightly on top
Eyes: Solid plastic

Tied by Dave Whitlock

WHITLOCK'S MULTICOLOR MUDDLER

Body: Gold Mylar tubing secured with red or orange thread
Wing: Yellow marabou and gold Flashabou over which is orange marabou and peacock herl with brown marabou on top
Collar: Black deer body hair over brown with orange deer body hair on the sides and yellow on the bottom
Head: Black, brown and orange deer body hair stacked over yellow, trimmed slightly rounded as shown and cemented on the bottom
Eyes: Solid plastic (optional)

Dave Whitlock ties his Multicolor (Marabou) Muddlers in many color combinations, but this one and a variation with a silver body and a white, yellow and olive marabou wing, seem to be the most common.

Tied by Dave Whitlock

Tied by Farrow Allen

WHITLOCK'S PRISMATIC SHINER

Hook:	Straight eye, 3X or 4X long stainless steel or nickle plated
Wing:	One or two white marabou plumes tied so the barbs are perpendicular to hook shank offering a broad flat silhouette Peacock herl is on top and a single grizzly hackle on each side
Body:	Pearl prismatic tape, trimmed as shown with the backing removed, is folded up from the bottom sandwiching the hook shank and the lower portion of the marabou wing, and finally secured at the head
Gills:	A strip of red prismatic tape or red hackle fluff
Cheeks:	Gray mallard flank
Eyes:	Hollow or solid plastic, or painted

Dave Whitlock began experimenting with prismatic tape in the mid 1970s and found it effective for "nearly all the thin, deep-bodied fish and minnows."

Tied by Dave Whitlock

WHITLOCK'S SHEEP SHAD

Hook:	Long shank stainless steel, bent as shown and tied hook point up
Throat:	A ball of fluorescent red yarn or dubbing over which is pearl crystal flash and white synthetic Fishair
Wing:	Pearlescent and pearl blue crystal flash over which is very pale gray lamb's wool and silver Flashabou
Sides:	On each side a strip of pearlescent Mylar, trimmed to a point, outside of which is a single pale-dun colored badger hackle
Cheeks:	Mallard breast feather, curving out
Eyes:	Solid plastic

Using fine lamb's wool, hackle and a little bit of synthetic flash, Whitlock has come up with a shad imitation that is translucent, easy to cast and very realistic. This fly has subtle colors and an elusive quality reminiscent of many baitfish.

Tied by Dave Whitlock

WHITLOCK'S SHEEP SUNFISH

Hook:	Long shank stainless steel, bent as shown and tied hook point up
Throat:	A ball of fluorescent red yarn or dubbing picked out, over which is yellow crystal flash and light yellow and orange lamb's wool
Wing:	Pearlescent yellow crystal flash over which is fine light yellow and orange-yellow lamb's wool over which is fine olive lamb's wool topped by peacock crystal flash
Sides:	Grizzly hackle dyed yellow
Cheeks:	A small ringneck pheasant back feather, curving out with a black lacquer "spot" painted as shown. The entire cheek is cemented to the yellow grizzly hackle
Eyes:	Solid plastic
Head:	Yellow

Part of a relatively-new series of baitfish imitations Dave Whitlock ties using fine translucent lamb's wool as the primary ingredient of the wing.

WIGGLE TAIL

Hook: Down eye, stainless steel, heavy wire
Tail: White marabou and pearlescent yellow or chartreuse crystal flash
Eyes: Lead, painted chartreuse with black pupils
Body: Chartreuse crystal chenille or Estaz chenille, heavy
Rib: Oval silver tinsel
Hackle: Pearl and silver Flashabou, or unravelled Mylar tubing, extending a little beyond the end of the tail
Head: Fluorescent green

Originally tied for Pacific salmon, but found to be extremely effective for bass. A close cousin to the Woolly Bugger (which see), it is popularly dressed in many colors using standard or fluorescent chenille as well as crystal chenille.

Tied by Doug Tucker-Eccher

WILKIE'S RUNT

Hook: Straight eye, wide gape
Underbody: Lead wire
Tail: White marabou
Body: White chenille
Rib: Flat silver tinsel
Wing: White marabou over which is peacock herl and a sparse mixture of silver Flashabou and pearl and silver crystal flash or Flashabou
Collar: Webby grizzly hackle
Eyes: Bead chain painted yellow with a black pupil
Head: White chenille and red thread
Note: All white and all yellow are the two most effective colors.

Wilkie's Runt has the basic fish-taking properties of the larger Wilkie's Shad (which see), but it's much easier to tie. Although it was initially designed for crappie fishing, it has been a reliable fly for all species of panfish and many bass as well.

Tied by Al Wilkie

WILKIE'S SHAD

Hook: Straight eye, wide gape or popper hook
Underbody: Lead wire
Body: White sparkle yarn
Rib: Gold wire
Wing: About six separate bunches of white marabou stripped from the stem and tied in bunches along the body at even intervals and secured with the gold wire. Over the marabou is peacock herl
Sides: A well marked teal flank feather on each side, cupped together covering the body and most of the marabou wing
Gills: A few turns of red floss (optional)
Eyes: Bead chain tied under the hook, painted yellow with black pupils. (If using a popper hook, the eyes will fit into the kink in the shank.)
Collar and head: White deer body hair spun and clipped as shown

Developed in 1980 by Al Wilkie, of Dallas, Texas, to imitate a thread-fin shad, one of the most prolific forage fish in Texas waters.

Tied by Al Wilkie

Baitfish

Tied by Doug Tucker-Eccher

WOBBLING-WOUNDED BLUEGILL

Hook: Straight eye, 6X long, rotated and tied at a 90° angle with the hook bend away from the tier

Tail: Chartreuse crystal flash over which are the butt ends of the blue Flashabou Minnow Body tubing used for the body

Underbody: Stainless steel, lead or aluminum tape, trimmed into the shape of a minnow

Body: Blue Flashabou Minnow Body tubing

Collar: Red hackle

Wing: Olive rabbit fur strip, secured at the head and tail

Eyes: Solid plastic

Note: A rattle chamber may be included in the underbody construction to create a Rattling-Wobbling-Wounded Bluegill.

Introduced by Doug Tucker-Eccher of The Bass Pond, who suggests substituting colors to match whatever minnow is to be imitated.

Tied by Tom Nixon

WOOLFOLK MINNOW

Hook: Straight eye, 3X or 4X long, or kinked shank popper hook

Tail: About 10 strands of partly unraveled 20 to 30 lb. test braided nylon fishing line

Fins: About 6 strands of partly unravelled 20 to 30 lb. test braided nylon fishing line

Body: Shaped balsa wood with grooves cut on either side to accommodate the fins, slotted and secured to the hook and over-wrapped, from the head to the tail, with same size braided fishing line as was used for the tail and fins. The completed body should be sealed with a coat or two of waterproof cement or varnish and then painted to look like whatever minnow you choose

Tom Nixon sent us this cleverly-constructed, floating minnow that is easily made from balsa wood and fishing line. Designed by Warren Woolfolk, of Lake Charles, Louisiana, for many years the Woolfolk Minnow has taken bass throughout the country.

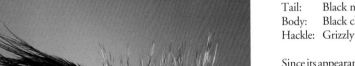

WOOLLY BUGGER

Hook: Down eye, 3X or 4X long

Tail: Black marabou

Body: Black chenille

Hackle: Grizzly

Since its appearance around the late 1970s, the Woolly Bugger has grown steadily in popularity and appeal. It is simple to tie, has unlimited variations and will catch nearly anything that's attracted to a moving bait. Although often classified as a streamer, Woolly Bugger designs can also successfully mimic most large swimming nymphs and leeches.

Tied by Karl Svendsen

WOOLLY BUGGER (CRYSTAL CHENILLE)

Hook: Down eye, 3X or 4X long
Tail: Cerise marabou
Body: Purple Crystal, Estaz or Glo-Brite chenille
Hackle: Cerise or cerise dyed grizzly
Note: As is the case with all Woolly Buggers, the color variations are limitless.

Almost as quickly as new synthetic tying materials appear in catalogs and local fly shops, "new" flies also appear. The variety of crystal chenilles available today has opened the door for many exciting - if not "new" - chenille-body fly patterns, often variations on existing patterns.

Tied by Karl Svendsen

WOUNDED MINNOW

Hook: Straight eye, wide gape
Tail: Two broad badger or grizzly hackles
Underbody: An optional split bead or ball of thread or foam to give shape to the head
Head and skirt: Natural or dyed dark bucktail over white bucktail, tied in with the tips facing forward and pulled back and tied off to form a fairly round bullet head
Eyes: Hollow plastic
Note: In the original pattern the head was coated with Pliobond rubber cement thinned with acetone. In this variation, epoxy cement has been used.

This is one of several patterns that were developed by the late Everett Drake of Indianapolis, Indiana. The Wounded Minnow was his best-known pattern and can be fished either as a bug or a streamer. This fly is sometimes called Drake's Slider.

Tied by Dick Stewart

ZONKER (PEARL & GRAY)

Hook: Down eye, 4X to 6X long, tied hook point up
Underbody: Aluminum or lead tape, folded over the the hook shank and trimmed into an exaggerated minnow shape
Body: Braided pearl Mylar tubing, pulled over the shaped underbody and secured at the tail with yellow thread
Wing: Natural gray rabbit fur strip, impaled through the hide and secured at the head
Collar: Yellow hackle
Note: As new pearlescent colors and sizes of braided Mylar tubing become available, the possibilities of tying larger and more realistic Zonkers increases.

From its introduction, the Zonker quickly gained the reputation of being a big-fish fly. Don Byford, who developed the Zonker, put the newly-introduced Mylar tubing to good use in constructing a large and very realistic baitfish imitation.

Tied by Dick Stewart

Tied by Farrow Allen

ADAMS

Hook:	Standard dry fly, light wire	Hackle:	Mixed grizzly and brown
Tail:	Mixed grizzly and brown hackle barbs	Head:	Black or gray
		Note:	Originally tied spent wing, though today the upright wing is more common.
Body:	Gray muskrat fur		
Wing:	Grizzly hackle tips		

A very productive "all-purpose" dry fly for luring panfish and bass to the surface, particularly useful if you happen to encounter a heavy mayfly hatch on which bass or panfish are feeding. Originally developed for trout, the Adams is one of those "good old flies" that imitates nothing in particular but a lot of things in general. Smallmouth bass and trout often live in different parts of the same river and a box of trout flies can sometimes be an asset.

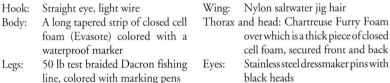

BETTS' FOAM DRAGONFLY

Hook:	Straight eye, light wire	Wing:	Nylon saltwater jig hair
Body:	A long tapered strip of closed cell foam (Evasote) colored with a waterproof marker	Thorax and head:	Chartreuse Furry Foam over which is a thick piece of closed cell foam, secured front and back
Legs:	50 lb test braided Dacron fishing line, colored with marking pens	Eyes:	Stainless steel dressmaker pins with black heads

Tied by John Betts

Using this basic construction any number of unsinkable adult flies can be imitated. John Betts designed this one to imitate the Green Darner, one of the most common dragonflies.

DAVE'S HOPPER

Hook:	Down eye, 2X or 3X long	Wing:	Mottled turkey wing quill, coated with vinyl cement, tied tent style
Tail:	Red hackle barbs over which is a loop of yellow poly yarn (or what ever body material you choose)	Legs:	Mottled stripped hackle stems or wing quill barbs, dyed yellow and knotted
Body:	Yellow poly yarn, acrylic or foam		
Hackle:	Brown, palmered forward and trimmed short	Head and collar:	Natural gray or gray dyed yellow deer body hair, spun and clipped square as shown
Underwing:	Brown bucktail dyed yellow		

Tied by Umpqua Feather Merchants

For Dave Whitlock, tying a fly to imitate a grasshopper has been an evolutional process. Dave's Hopper represents only one stage in a long line of flies which began in the early 1950s when he modified a Joe's Hopper with a spun deer-hair head and called it a Muddler Hopper.

DOUG'S HAIR MOTH

Hook:	Straight eye, wide gape	Wing:	Light elk over which is gray Z-lon, tied spent
Tail:	Light elk body hair		
Abdomen:	White rabbit and gray chinchilla rabbit fur, mixed to a dirty white, tied full and flattened	Thorax:	Chinchilla rabbit fur with the guard hairs
		Antennae:	Dun hackle tips

Doug Tucker-Eccher of The Bass Pond in Littleton, Colorado, designed this very realistic moth imitation. Since moths are nocturnal, they usually work best after dark. Doug's Hair Moth looks so convincing it will draw a hungry bass to the surface most anytime of day.

Tied by Doug Tucker-Eccher

ELK HAIR CADDIS (BROWN)

Hook: Standard dry, light wire
Body: Brown dubbing
Hackle: Brown, palmered over the body
Rib: Fine gold wire

Wing: Light tan elk body hair
Head: Butt ends of the wing clipped short, extending over the eye of the hook

Although designed for trout, this caddisfly imitation is one of the small insect representations which warmwater anglers should include in their arsenals. Most smallmouth bass can be drawn to the surface by the commotion of an insect fluttering across the water, trying to escape the surface and become airborne. Al Troth's Elk Hair Caddis works well in those instances or whenever caddisflies are hatching and bass are around.

Tied by Jack Russell

FEATHERWING MOTH

Hook: Standard dry, light wire
Underbody: Closed-cell foam
Body: Tan chenille wound over the foam underbody

Wings: Two rounded secondary wing feathers from a goose, duck or pheasant, tied flat on top
Antennae: The stems of the wing feathers

It must be some 35 years ago that I took my first bass on a Featherwing Moth. The design was undoubtedly inspired by a drawing in Ed Leonard's book *Flies*, and except for the difficulties in casting this air-resistant creature, the fly instilled a feeling of confidence. Cast this bug to the edge of a lily pad, let it sit quietly for up to a minute, then quiver your rod tip until the fly vibrates on the surface - and hold on.

Tied by Dick Stewart

FOAM BEETLE

Hook: Standard dry, light wire
Body: Peacock herl
Legs: A turn of starling hackle

Shellback and head: Black closed-cell poly (floating) foam cut to shape, pulled forward and tied off with red thread

The introduction of the new polyethylene closed-cell foams into the arena of fly tying has opened the door for development of many simple, and other not-so-simple bugs that are rugged and virtually unsinkable. For sunfish we've found the foam beetle to be a terrific floating fly that you should cast around old logs, branches and such.

Tied by Dick Stewart

FOAM CATERPILLAR

Hook: Straight eye, wide gape
Tail: Yellow rubber hackle
Body: Yellow closed-cell (Polycelon) foam, folded around the hook shank

Rib: Tying thread to define body segments
Hackle: Grizzly
Eyes: Hollow plastic
Antennae: Yellow rubber hackle

Originated by David Lucca, a school teacher and commercial fly tier from Stanchfield, Minnesota. Lucca likes to tie many of his bass and panfish patterns using foam bodies. "When used correctly, Polycelon (closed-cell foam) floats better than any material I have tried."

Tied by David Lucca

Insects

Tied by David Lucca

FOAM DRAGONFLY

Hook: Straight eye, wide gape
Extended body: Gray closed cell (Polycelon) foam (leave enough foam to pull forward over the dubbed thorax and fold back to form a head)
Rib: Bright blue thread
Wing: Fine deer body hair tied spent, over which is pearl crystal flash
Thorax: Gray dubbing around the wings
Head and back: Front end of foam used for the abdomen pulled forward and folded back to form a head, and tied off behind the eye of the hook
Eyes: Hollow plastic

This convincing dragonfly imitation from David Lucca is durable and nearly impossible to sink. Because dragonflies appear in so many colors, it is convenient to have a good supply of marking pens on hand to customize your body colors.

Tied by Umpqua Feather Merchants

GODDARD CADDIS

Hook: Light wire, standard dry
Body: Natural deer body hair, spun and trimmed into a form resembling a winged adult caddisfly
Antennae: Brown hackle stems with the barbs removed
Hackle: Brown

Caddisflies of one kind or another are abundant in many lakes, ponds and rivers that contain bass and panfish. This fly design is credited to John Goddard and is used for fishing in both fast and still waters. For more realism the original pattern included a twisted loop of olive dubbing on the underside of the deer-hair body. This simplified version works well for bass and panfish in every type of water.

Tied by Dick Stewart

HARD-BODIED ANT (BLACK)

Hook: Standard dry, light wire
Abdomen: A ball of thread, lacquered black
Legs: A turn or two of black hackle
Thorax: A small ball of thread, lacquered black (be sure to leave a space between the abdomen and thorax, to provide a strong ant silhouette)

Throughout most of the season ants are available to panfish. When ants are mating, however they grow wings, congregate in huge swarms, mate in the air and eventually fall into the water, causing feeding frenzies. During these periods, the body should be made to float and a pair of spent wings should be added to the basic dressing.

Tied by Farrow Allen

IMPROVED SOFA PILLOW

Hook: Down eye, 2X or 3X long, light wire
Tail: Elk body hair
Body: Burnt orange yarn or dubbing
Rib: Orange thread or gold wire
Body hackle: Brown or furnace
Wing: Elk body hair
Hackle: Brown
Head: Brown

This is a great looking fly that drives bass wild when it's skated across the surface of a still pool. When fished in this way a bass doesn't get much of a chance to think; it either turns and hits the fly or just lets it go by. Originated as an imitation of western stoneflies, the Improved Sofa Pillow is simply a good all-purpose dry fly for smallmouth bass.

JIMMINY CRICKET

Hook: Straight eye, wide gape
Antennae: Black rubber hackle
Body: Strip of black closed cell (Poly-celon) foam laid on top of the hook shank, (extending over the eye to fold back later and form the head) secured and segmented at intervals with black thread

Rib: Sparse black dubbing (optional)
Wing: Dark mottled turkey tail, over which is a short collar of black deer body hair
Legs: Black rubber hackle, knotted once
Head: Black foam folded forward and back and tied off
Eyes: Hollow plastic (optional)

This is a rugged cricket that can withstand the capture of many bass. Its originator, David Lucca, is a highly versatile fly tier who is as comfortable tying small delicate trout flies as he is at manufacturing unique foam bass and panfish creations.

Tied by David Lucca

JOE'S HOPPER

Hook: Down eye, 2X long
Tail: Red hackle barbs over which is a loop of yellow poly yarn
Body: Yellow poly yarn, dubbing or foam
Body hackle: Brown, palmered forward, trimmed completely on the side,

and the length of the hook gape on the top and bottom
Wings: Sections of mottled turkey wing quills that have been treated with vinyl cement
Hackle: Mixed brown and grizzly

Although it was named originally the "Michigan Hopper," this fly is best known as Joe's Hopper, having been popularized by the late Joe Brooks. For years it was one of the few hopper flies that was commercially available. While still a good pattern, it has generally been replaced by patterns tied with deer-hair heads.

Tied by Umpqua Feather Merchants

LETORT CRICKET

Hook: Down eye, 2X long
Body: Black fur
Wing: Black wing quill section, tied flat over the body

Head: Black deer body hair, spun and trimmed to shape, leaving a few hairs uncut on the sides and top

This and the following Letort Hopper were designed by Ed Shenk of Carlisle, Pennsylvania. Originally tied for summer trout fishing, the Letort Cricket in larger sizes is just as good for bass and panfish. Best fished on warm summer evenings when crickets are most active.

Tied by Ed Shenk

LETORT HOPPER

Hook: Down eye, 2X long
Body: Yellow fur
Wing: Mottled turkey wing quill section, V-notched and tied flat over the

body
Head: Natural deer body hair, spun and trimmed to shape leaving some hairs uncut on the sides and top

Ed Shenk's Letort Hopper is a good summer pattern for spooky bass in clear water. When the sun is high and smallmouth are hiding in cover, tight against grassy shorelines, a well-presented Letort Hopper can be a most effective fly.

Tied by Ed Shenk

Insects

Tied by Farrow Allen

MOSQUITO

Hook:	Standard dry, light wire	Rib:	Fine silver wire, counter-wrapped
Tail:	Grizzly hackle barbs		(optional)
Body:	One light and one dark strand of	Wing:	Grizzly hackle tips
	moose mane, wound together	Hackle:	Grizzly

On the local bluegill pond, mosquitoes and summer evenings go together. It's difficult to dispute the wisdom of tying on this fly at dusk when mosquitoes are beginning to hatch. When the mosquitoes begin to bite, the bluegills aren't far behind.

Tied by Joe Messinger, Jr.

NITEHUMMER

Hook:	Straight eye, wide gape		cut on the side
Tail:	Black deer body hair	Wing:	Black deer body hair
Body:	Pale yellow and bright yellow over	Throat:	Black deer body hair, well ce-
	white deer body hair, trimmed as		mented
	shown including several notches		

The Nitehummer imitates a giant nocturnal moth and was developed during the 1920s by Joe Messinger, Sr., who also brought us Messinger's Bucktail Frog (which see).

Tied by Dick Stewart

WHITE HAIR MOTH

Hook:	Down eye, 2X long		entire upper half of the body
Body:	White deer body hair, spun and	Head:	White deer body hair, spun and
	trimmed to a cigar shape		trimmed as shown
Wing:	White deer body hair over the	Eyes:	Hollow plastic

This simple deer-hair moth represents a design that has been with us for many years. It's still effective when fished at dusk, cast above an unsuspecting bass, allowed to sit motionless and then twitched and made to quiver like a live moth trapped in the surface film.

Tied by Dick Stewart

WHITLOCK'S BASS HOPPER

Hook:	Down eye, 3X or 4X long		crystal flash. On each side are 2
Body:	Yellow polypropylene yarn		badger hackles dyed yellow and
Hackle:	Badger hackle dyed yellow		splayed outward
	palmered over the body	Collar and head: Natural brown deer body	
Wing:	2 or 3 yellow hackles tied flat, over		hair dyed gold on top and yellow-
	which is sparse yellow dyed brown		dyed deer body hair on the bottom
	bucktail and pearlescent yellow	Legs:	Yellow or chartreuse rubber hackle

Dave Whitlock recently designed this grasshopper pattern specifically for bass.

WHITLOCK'S DAMSEL

Hook: Straight eye, wide gape
Wing: Kingfisher blue and natural deer body hair, relatively short
Legs: Blue rubber hackle (optional)
Underbody: Foam secured to the hook to build up the thorax and provide flotation
Extended abdomen, thorax and head: Dark blue bucktail for the back and kingfisher blue bucktail underneath, tied with the tips facing forward and pulled back over the foam underbody, secured to the hook shank with gray thread and segmented with blue thread wraps
Eyes: Prismatic hollow plastic

Depending on the size and color you choose for tying this Dave Whitlock pattern, it can imitate a wide variety of adult damselflies or dragonflies.

Tied by Umpqua Feather Merchants

WHITLOCK'S SPENT KRYSTAL DRAGON

Hook: Straight eye, wide gape
Wing: 2 bunches of pearl crystal flash tied spent and marked with black stripes
Legs: Speckled tan-olive rubber hackle
Underbody: Closed-cell foam
Extended abdomen, thorax and head: Light tan-olive bucktail over white bucktail. On each upper and lower side is a strand of wide pearl Mylar, all of this tied bullet-head style with the tips tied forward and then pulled back over and around the foam underbody, segmented and secured with wraps of fluorescent green thread
Eyes: Prismatic hollow plastic
Note: Mylar is optional and body details may be applied with a marking pen

Dave Whitlock has shown us here how to use synthetic materials to capture the iridescence of an adult dragonfly.

Tied by Umpqua Feather Merchants

WULFF, GRAY

Hook: Down eye, 1X or 2X long, light or standard wire
Tail: Natural brown bucktail
Body: Gray muskrat fur or yarn
Wing: Brown bucktail
Hackle: Blue dun

This is one of Lee Wulff's patterns from the early 1930s. In fact, the Gray Wulff is probably the very first fly of the original "Wulff" series. Although it was first tied for use as a trout fly in fast water, it floats well and has fooled many bass. This is a favorite fly for lake fishing during the hatches of the huge, lumbering *Hexagenia* mayflies which can be so numerous they trigger a feeding frenzy.

Tied by Bill Franke

WULFF, WHITE

Hook: Down eye, 1X or 2X long, light or standard wire
Tail: White bucktail or calftail
Body: White fur or yarn
Wing: White bucktail or calftail
Hackle: Badger

This is another one of Lee Wulff's original trout patterns that has aided in the demise of many bass. During the summer, when hatches of large mayflies frequently occur at dusk, bass and panfish can often be fooled by this or the darker Gray Wulff. Although bass can be moody and uncooperative, they seem generally less selective than trout, and will hit a dry fly that approximates the size and color of whatever is hatching.

Tied by Bill Franke

Nymphs

BIG UGLY

Tied by Ian James

Hook:	Down eye, heavy wire	Head:	White ostrich herl
Underbody:	Lead wire (optional)	Note:	Brush and fluff up the body with a
Tag:	A few turns of pearl Flashabou		toothbrush after the dubbing has
Body:	Gray fox fur with guard hairs		been applied. The protruding
	(taken from the side of the belly)		guard hairs will help keep the hen
Collar:	Speckled hen hackle		hackle from sticking to the body.

Developed by Ian James of Guelph, Ontario, the Big Ugly is a popular bass nymph throughout southern Ontario. It is usually tied weighted for river fishing, but unweighted for ponds where it is fished over shallow weed beds and rocky ledges.

BITCH CREEK

Hook:	Down eye, 3X or 4X long	Legs:	Brown hackle over thorax
Underbody:	A peice of heavy lead wire on	Rib:	Gold wire counter-wrapped over
	each side of the hook shank		the brown hackle for strength (op-
Tail:	Two strands of white rubber hackle		tional)
Abdomen:	Woven black and orange che-	Antennae:	Two strands of white rubber
	nille on rear ½ of hook shank		hackle
Thorax:	Black chenille		

Originally tied for trout as a generic stonefly nymph imitation.

CASUAL DRESS

Hook:	Down eye, 2X long		"noodle" of muskrat fur, dubbed
Underbody:	Lead wire under the thorax		with a spinning loop
Tail:	Muskrat guard hairs with about	Collar:	Muskrat guard hairs
	half the underfur left in	Head:	Black ostrich herl or rabbit fur
Thorax and abdomen: A thick tapered			

This is Jacques Juneau's bass fly variation of a nymph originated for trout by Polly Rosborough.

Tied by Jacques Juneau

CLOUSER HELLGRAMMITE

Tied by Bob Clouser

Hook:	Down eye, 2X long	Legs:	Grizzly hackle palmered over the
Tail:	Short bunch of black rabbit fur		body
Extended body:	Black rabbit fur strip	Back:	Black Furry Foam
Body:	Black rabbit fur	Antennae:	Black Furry Foam cut to shape

Designed to be fished dead drift in a natural manner. The extended rabbit strip abdomen moves about in the water currents in a way that closely resembles a live hellgrammite.

CLOUSER SWIMMING NYMPH

Hook: Down eye, 1X or 2X long
Tail: Copper Flashabou, surrounded by brown marabou
Abdomen: Rusty-claret dubbing
Thorax: Rusty-claret dubbing
Legs: Brown speckled hen body hackle, wrapped over the thorax
Wingcase: Peacock herl
Head: Fluorescent red

This is Bob Clouser's all-purpose swimming nymph that represents a variety of the large nymphs upon which bass feed.

Tied by Bob Clouser

DRAGON FLY NYMPH

Hook: Down eye, 3X long
Underbody: Lead wire (optional)
Abdomen: Black yarn or fur, applied thick and heavy
Legs: Black braided casting line, knotted to form leg joints
Thorax and head: Black yarn or fur

This is a very simple-to-tie yet very believable dragonfly imitation originated by Montana's Gary Saindon, author of *The Off-Season Angler*.

Tied by Gary Saindon

DRAGONFLY NYMPH MUDDLER

Hook: Down eye, 3X long
Tail: Olive dyed marabou, cut off short
Body: Olive yarn or dubbing
Wing: Two grizzly hackles dyed olive and tied flat over the body
Collar: Olive deer body hair
Head: Olive deer body hair, spun and clipped flat on the top and bottom, and lacquered in front and on the bottom

Originally tied in smaller sizes for trout fishing, this "nymph-muddler" comes from Ed Rief of Bangor, Maine. Rief describes it as being most effective in June, when smallmouth feed in the shallows on dragonfly nymphs.

Tied by Ed Rief

DREDGEBUG (BROWN)

Hook: Down eye, 2X or 3X long
Underbody: Lead wire, if desired
Body: Peacock herl, brown wool or dubbing, tied full
Legs: Soft brown hen or grouse hackle
          applied as a collar
Wing: Dyed brown mallard flank or similar, folded tent-like over the body
Head: Brown chenille over optional lead eyes

The Dredgebug is a generic imitation of a dragonfly nymph that combines some of the design features of the Muddler and the Hornberg (both very popular flies, but neither one is fast-sinking.) The Dredgebug series was first introduced by Dick Stewart in the early 1980s in *Fly Tyer* magazine. Because dragonflies are found in many colors, this fly is successful tied in many shades of olive, brown and gray.

Tied by Dick Stewart

Nymphs

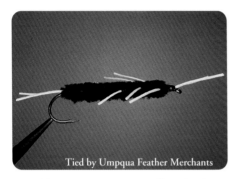

Tied by Umpqua Feather Merchants

GIRDLE BUG

Hook:	Down eye, 4X to 6X long	Body:	Black chenille
Underbody:	Lead wire wrapped around hook shank or tied along the sides	Antennae:	Two strips of white or gray rubber hackle
Tail:	Two strips white or gray rubber hackle	Note:	The Ugly Bug, Girdle Bug and Rubberlegs are all similar patterns featuring a chenille body, and legs, tail and antennae of rubber hackle in a variety of colors.
Legs:	Three sets of white or gray rubber hackle spaced evenly down the side of the hook shank		

Originally the Girdle Bug was tied as an imitation of a large black stonefly nymph. It is readily taken by smallmouth feeding in fast water.

GREEN DARNER NYMPH

Hook:	Down eye, 3X long	Body:	Olive yarn or dubbing, tapering up towards the head
Underbody:	Strips of heavy lead wire secured to the top of the hook shank to help keep the hook point up	Head:	Brown yarn or dubbing
		Hackle:	Grizzly dyed yellow palmered over the body
Tail:	Light olive marabou		

Tied by Dana Griffin

This nymph was designed by Dana Griffin of Gainesville, Florida, to imitate the larval form of a very common dragonfly. Effective on panfish and bass alike, in still water it should be fished with short darting retrieves interspersed with long pauses. In rivers and streams it is most effective fished dead drift.

HARE'S EAR NYMPH

Hook:	Down eye, 1X or 2X long	Thorax:	Hare's mask fur with guard hairs, applied heavily
Tail:	Hare's mask fur with guard hairs		
Abdomen:	Hare's mask fur with guard hairs	Wingcase:	Goose wing quill segment
Rib:	Oval gold tinsel	Legs:	Fur from the thorax, picked out

This variation of the old English wet fly is a fine generic nymph imitation for smallmouth feeding in moving water. In fact, this is simply a great fly and there is hardly a fly fisher anywhere who doesn't have a Hare's Ear Nymph, weighted or unweighted, in his fly box. Tied in smaller sizes it is effective on panfish. This fly is often called a Gold-ribbed Hare's Ear Nymph.

HELLGRAMMITE

Hook:	Down eye, 6X long, slightly bent as shown	Gills:	Natural black schlappen, trimmed flush on the top and bottom and short on the sides
Underbody:	Heavy lead wire on the sides of the hook shank		
Tail:	The tip of a natural black hen body feather or similar	Thorax:	Black and brown fur, picked out
		Legs:	Three turns of black schlappen, trimmed flush on top and bottom
Abdomen:	A mixture of black and brown fur, roughened	Wingcase:	Black wing quill segment, treated with vinyl cement, folded forward and back forming a head as well
Rib:	Black floss followed by gold wire along the front edge of the floss	Feelers:	Black goose biots

Tied by Farrow Allen

This Hellgrammite variation was tied by Farrow Allen in the late 1970s for the Lower Lamoille River above Arrowhead Lake in Milton, Vermont. During the early summer this boulder strewn stretch of the Lamoille is loaded with hellgrammites and smallmouth bass.

MONTANA

Hook: Down eye, 3X long
Underbody: Lead wire (optional)
Tail: Black hackle barbs
Abdomen: Black chenille
Thorax: Yellow chenille
Legs: Black hackle
Wingcase: Black chenille

A popular western nymph that is very effective for smallmouth in eastern freestone rivers where stonefly nymphs are commonplace.

Tied by Umpqua Feather Merchants

MURRAY'S HELLGRAMMITE

Hook: Down eye, 2X long
Underbody: Lead wire
Tail (extended body): Black ostrich herl
Body: Black chenille
Hackle: Very soft dark dun, palmered over the body
Feelers: Black rubber hackle
Note: Lead eyes may be applied at the head instead of using a lead wire underbody.

Developed in 1978 by Harry Murray of Edinburg, Virginia, author of *Fly Fishing for Smallmouth Bass*. This fly is designed to simulate the natural movement of a live hellgrammite in fast water. The ostrich herl moves in a manner that mimics the way a natural hellgrammite swims in the current.

Tied by Harry Murray

MURRAY'S STRYMPH

Hook: Down eye, 2X or 3X long
Underbody: Lead wire
Tail: Olive ostrich herl
Body: Olive rabbit fur
Collar: Brown speckled hen hackle
Note: Effective tied in black and cream.

This pattern was developed in 1980 by Harry Murray and can be fished effectively upstream as a nymph or down-and-across like a streamer. Murray credits Ed Shenk of Carlisle, Pennsylvania, for developing the concept of fur-body streamers, but Murray, who owns a fly-fishing shop in Virginia, worked out the details of the Strymph series.

Tied by Harry Murray

OSCAR'S HEXAGENIA NYMPH

Tail: Short soft brown hackle and three or four ringneck pheasant tail barbs
Underbody: Dental floss built into a tapered body and flattened with pliers
Abdomen: Cream sparkle yarn
Rib: Oval gold tinsel
Abdomen top: Pheasant tail or mottled turkey, lacquered
Gills: A gray stem of down from a partridge or pheasant, trimmed and folded over the top of the abdomen before pulling the turkey or pheasant tail over
Thorax: Orange sparkle yarn
Hackle: Brown hackle palmered over thorax and trimmed across bottom
Wingcase: Lacquered pheasant tail or mottled turkey
Head and eyes: Orange thread around 15 lb. test melted monofilament eyes

Tied by Oscar Feliu

The nymph of the *Hexagenia limbata* mayfly can be an important source of food to panfish and bass. In lakes where *Hexagenia* exist, they are often abundant and begin hatching at dark, continuing to hatch well into the evening.

Nymphs

Tied by Phil Camera

RIVER WITCH

Hook: Down eye, 4X long
Tail: Black marabou
Underbody: White wet-fly foam, over-wrapped with flat pearl Mylar
Abdomen: Woven Larva Lace, black on top and clear underneath
Thorax: Black chenille
Hackle: Several turns of soft black hackle over the thorax

The River Witch was originated as a trout fly by Phil Camera of Phil's Tackle in Woodland Park, Colorado. Over the years it has proven its worth on both largemouth and smallmouth bass. Obviously, this durable fly can be tied in any color desired.

Tied by Dick Stewart

TED'S STONEFLY

Hook: Down eye, 3X long
Tail: Goose biots, dyed brown
Abdomen: Brown chenille
Thorax: Orange chenille
Legs: Brown (or black) hackle
Wingcase: Brown chenille

This simple and effective nymph is credited to outdoor writer Ted Trueblood. It is a good stonefly imitation in freestone rivers where bass and stoneflies abound, and often the brown color outproduces the similarly constructed black Montana nymph (which see).

Tied by Umpqua Feather Merchants

WHITLOCK'S DAMSEL NYMPH (BROWN)

Hook: Down eye, 3X or 4X long
Tail: Brown marabou
Abdomen: Brown fur
Rib: Gold wire
Eyes: Melted monofilament
Thorax: Brown fur
Legs: Red-brown speckled grouse or hen
Wingcase: Brown nylon raffia brought forward over the thorax and secured both behind and in front of the eyes

Damselfly nymphs, like Dave Whitlock's imitation, have long, slender abdomens, short thoraxes and big eyes. They are aggressive swimmers and are often active during daylight hours. They are generally smaller than dragonfly nymphs, but are usually more abundant.

WHITLOCK'S DRAGON NYMPH (OLIVE)

Hook: Salmon wet
Abdomen: Olive fur over rear half of the hook, heavily built up at the rear
Back: Olive nylon raffia over the abdomen
Rib: Gold wire over the back and abdomen
Thorax and head: Olive fur over front half of the hook, in two segments
Legs: A bunch of soft grizzly hackle barbs dyed olive, extending between the segments on each side
Eyes: Melted monofilament
Wingcase and head: Olive nylon raffia in two segments secured over the abdomen and head

Dragonfly nymphs inhabit the same ponds and slow-moving rivers as damselflies. Their bodies are usually stout and may be as much as two inches long, in colors ranging from tan and olive to brown and gray.

WHITLOCK'S HELLGRAMMITE

Hook: Straight eye, 6X long, bent as shown to ride upside-down
Tail: Goose biots, dyed charcoal and separated by a ball of olive-dun fur
Abdomen: Olive-dun fur
Abdomen top: Charcoal nylon raffia
Rib: Copper wire

Thorax: Olive dun fur
Legs: Dark speckled hen, grouse or similar body feather
Wingcase: Charcoal nylon raffia, in three segments
Antennae: Goose biots, dyed charcoal

As some bait fishermen know, in many rivers the hellgrammite is an important food source for bass. To be most effective the fly must be fished near the stream bottom. Tied with the hook point up this design by Dave Whitlock allows you to present the fly deep with less risk of it becoming snagged.

Tied by Umpqua Feather Merchants

WHITLOCK'S RED SQUIRREL NYMPH

Hook: Straight eye, 2X long
Tail: Red fox squirrel body hair and underfur
Underbody: Lead wire under the thorax
Abdomen: Red fox squirrel belly blended with a similarly colored synthetic dubbing like Antron
Rib: Pearl Flashabou

Legs: Tan or tan-speckled rubber hackle
Thorax: Dark hair clipped from the back of a red fox squirrel and blended with a similarly colored synthetic like Antron
Legs: Dark speckled hen back, palmered over the thorax
Antennae: Tan or tan-speckled rubber hackle

Dave Whitlock designed this nymph and it's proved to be a great all-purpose fly for many species of gamefish. It's often tied in larger sizes for bass.

Tied by Jack Russell

WOOLY WORM (YELLOW)

Hook: Down eye, 3X long
Tail: Red wool yarn
Body: Yellow chenille
Hackle: Grizzly, palmered over the body
Rib: Gold wire, counter-wrapped for

strength (optional)
Note: Wooly worms are tied with a variety of body colors, although the red yarn tail and grizzly hackle usually remain constant.

Tied in many colors, the Wooly Worm has been popular for years in both lakes and streams for a variety of fish from bluegills to steelhead. It works well for smallmouth bass in rivers when cast upstream and rolled deep along the bottom.

Tied by Farrow Allen

YUK BUG

Hook: Down eye, 4X to 6X long
Underbody: Lead wire
Tail: Gray squirrel tail
Body: Black chenille
Legs: Three white rubber hackle legs

evenly spaced along the side of the body, slanting backward
Hackle: Light badger, tied in by the tip and palmered forward with an extra wrap or two at the head

Although this pattern was developed as a bottom-dredging nymph for trout holding in fast water, bass and panfish find it equally appealing. In lakes and ponds it can be cast towards shore along rocky ledges and retrieved slowly along the bottom with great results.

Tied by Umpqua Feather Merchants

Panfish Flies

Tied by Michele Lemieux

BABY SEAL

Hook: Straight eye, standard wire
Tag: Flat gold tinsel
Body: Orange seal fur or substitute, tied full and picked out
Collar: Speckled grouse, partridge or similar
Head: Fluorescent red

The Baby Seal is a simple soft-hackle, full-bodied wet fly from Canadian tier Michele Lemieux of Trois-Rivières. Lemieux ties it in many colors, but the orange version is one of his best for Quebec bluegills.

Tied by Blane Holtz

BBX

Hook: Down eye, 1X long
Body: Red closed-cell foam, pre-formed or trimmed to shape as shown
Legs: White rubber hackle
Hackle: Grizzly
Note: The red-bodied BBX represents the original dressing, but other colors may work just as well

Blane Holtz from Ontario, Canada, introduced this beetle in the late 1980s to fool trout; but we have found that it works even better on panfish.

Tied by Farrow Allen

BIVISIBLE (BROWN)

Hook: Standard dry, light wire
Tail: Two brown hackle tips, each curving out, or brown hackle barbs
Body: Three to six stiff hackles tied in at the rear and palmered forward tightly. At the front add one white hackle
Note: Effectively tied with badger, black, grizzly or bright dyed hackle.

Developed for trout during the 1930s, bushy bivisibles float high on their hackles and are good "searching" patterns for bluegills in the shallows.

Tied by Tim England

BRASS WONDER (OLIVE)

Hook: Down eye, standard wire
Head: Brass bead, worked over the pinched down barb of the hook and secured in place with red thread
Tail: Dyed olive rabbit fur
Body: Dyed olive rabbit fur
Sides: Chartreuse crystal flash extending beyond the tail and along the body
Rib: Clear monofilament binding the crystal flash along the sides

This all-fur panfish fly is part of a series of bead-head patterns called "Brass Wonders" developed by Tim England. They perform like jigs but are effortless to cast.

Tied by Tim England

BRASS WONDER (SILVER)

Hook: Down eye, standard wire
Head: Nickle-plated brass bead, worked over the pinched down barb of the hook and secured in place with red thread
Throat: Peacock herl
Wing: Gray marabou over which is pearl crystal flash and white marabou

This bright, flashy little panfish pattern is named the Silver Minnow and is part of Tim England's "Brass Wonder" series that began in 1975. In shallow water, the Silver Minnow cast along shoreline cover can be deadly.

Tied by Jim Stewart

BRIM BUG EYE

Hook: Down eye, 1X long
Tail: White rubber hackle and red crystal flash
Body: Black chenille
Shellback: Braided silver tinsel
Hackle: Purple, palmered over the body and shellback
Head: Rose or black with silver bead chain eyes

Jim Stewart notes that bluegills will go out of their way to catch up with this fly.

Tied by Tom Lentz

Tied by Tom Lentz

Tied by Bill Bell

BRIM FLY (GRAY)

Hook: Down eye, standard wire
Tail: White marabou
Underbody: Lead wire
Body: Gray chenille
Legs: White rubber hackle
Shellback: Variegated black and brown chenille
Head: Red

Tom Lentz calls this his number-one brim fly for the 1990 season," and that's from a fisherman who spends more time chasing bluegills than anyone we know. Lentz says it is "also catches bass and specs (crappie)."

BRIM SPECIAL

Hook: Down eye, standard wire
Underbody: Lead wire
Tail: Fluorescent green marabou
Body: Fluorescent green chenille
Shellback: Variegated fluorescent green and black chenille
Legs: White rubber hackle, pulled back
Head: Variegated fluorescent green and black chenille

Tom Lentz derived his Brim Special from a pattern called the Hum Bug, one of a series of panfish flies from The Gaines Company, a manufacturer of fly-rod popping bugs.

BUMBLE BEE

Hook: Down eye, standard wire
Body: Alternating black and yellow segments of spun deer body hair
Wing: Natural tan deer body hair

This is George Richey's favorite bluegill fly. George and his brother Dave Richey are well known for their midwest steelhead flies and books on steelhead fishing. Dave, who does most of the tying, is allergic to deer hair and had Bill Bell tie these for him.

Tied by Tom Nixon

Tied by Jack Ellis

Tied by Tom Nixon

CAJUN COACHMAN

Hook: Down eye, 1X long
Underbody: Lead wire
Body: Rear section: Red floss, tied well down the bend of the hook
       Front section: Peacock herl
Throat: Brown hackle barbs
Wing: A single broad black-and-white barred woodduck flank feather, folded in half lengthwise before being tied in

This bluegill wet-fly pattern is a favorite of Tom Nixon's when he fishes the large marsh impoundments, creeks and bayous of Louisiana.

CATALPA WORM

Hook: Down eye, 4X long, slightly humped
Tail: Black goose biots
Body: Cream or pale yellow lamb's wool
Back: Black chenille, pulled over like a shellback
Hackle: Black, stripped on one side and clipped closely on the other after wrapping over the body

Jack Ellis of Woodville, Texas, ties this fly to imitate one of many tree-dwelling, leaf-eating, smooth-body worms that fall from deciduous trees bordering southern ponds and creeks. They often provide a tasty meal for hungry bream.

CATERPILLAR

Hook: Down eye, 6X long
Body: Natural deer body hair spun and clipped into a cylindrical shape
Hackle: Grizzly, palmered over the deer hair body after it's been clipped

Tom Nixon sent this fly and says that it should be tied in any size or color that reflects local caterpillar populations. He also suggests practicing your side arm delivery so you can place the fly "far back under low hanging tree limbs where the real bull bream hang out."

Panfish Flies

Tied by Dick Stewart

CHENILLE BUG (GRAY)

Hook: Down eye, standard wire
Tail: Grizzly hackle barbs
Body: Gray chenille
Collar: Grizzly hackle
Head: Red

Tie this fly with any color hackle and chenille that looks good to you. It's a basic panfish wet fly perfect for beginning fly tiers. Crystal and Estaz chenilles, fluorescent or tinsel chenilles, all add a bit more sparkle and range to the possible ways of tying this bug.

Tied by Tom Nixon

DEEP BLACK

Hook: Down eye, standard wire
Body: Embossed gold tinsel
Wing: Two black hackles, curving out
Collar: Black hackle
Head: Small split shot, crimped flat and glued onto the hook in front of the collar, painted black
Eyes: Yellow with a red pupil

Tom Nixon designed the Deep Black for crappie and bluegill fishing at spawning time when "a quick retrieve works best." At other times it works for probing deep cover.

Tied by Dick Stewart

DEVIL BUG (RED)

Hook: Down eye, 1X long
Body: Red chenille
Tail, shellback and head: Natural light or white deer body hair, secured front and back with red thread
Note: A popular variation uses a peacock herl body with natural deer hair.

This simple and effective fly is also known as a Cooper Bug or Doodle Bug. It is easy and inexpensive to tie and can be constructed using a wide variety of colors of chenille and deer hair.

Tied by Jack Ellis

FATHEAD DIVER

Hook: Straight eye, standard wire
Wing: Short gray squirrel tail over which is red marabou followed by brown marabou fibers
Head and collar: Natural deer body hair, spun and trimmed as shown, like a Dahlberg Diver and well cemented except for the collar
Note: Jack Ellis ties this in many different color combinations.

Jack Ellis developed the Fathead Diver during a period of drought out of need for a small fly that would "...fish like a bug in the weeds and like a streamer in open water."

Tied by George Kesel

GILL BUGGER

Hook: Straight eye, wide gape
Bead head: A green glass bead, slipped over the point of the hook and secured
Tail: Two dark and two light green rubber hackles
Skirt: Olive deer body hair
Body: Olive and yellow deer body hair
Legs: Same as tail
Wing: Two olive grizzly hackle tips, tied spent and olive deer body hair, fanned over the top
Head: Olive deer body hair
Eyes: Hollow plastic

Originated by John Gantner who says that big bluegills like this fly in the surface film.

Tied by Tom Lentz

GILL GETTER

Hook: Down eye, standard wire
Underbody: Lead wire
Tail: Moose mane
Legs: White rubber hackle
Body: Fluorescent green chenille
Shellback: Moose mane that is the continuation of mane used for the tail
Head: Fluorescent green

Big bluegills are most inclined to seek shelter along ledges, pilings and deep drop-offs. The Gill Getter was designed as a nymph to be fished deep and slow in these and similar types of structure. Lentz considers it to be one of his very best bluegill flies.

Tied by George Kesel

Tied by Lorraine Close

Tied by Lorraine Close

GILL SLIDER

Hook: Straight eye, wide gape
Tail: 4 gray rubber hackles
Body: Closed cell foam
Wing: Two grizzly hackle tips
Head and collar: Natural deer body hair
           secured in front of a bead (previ-
           ously slipped over the hook shank)
           with the tips pointing forward,
           pulled back over the bead to form
           a bullet head
Eyes: Hollow plastic

John Gantner designed the Gill Slider in various colors for fishing in the surface film.

GRUBBY GERT

Hook: Straight eye, standard wire
Tail: Grass green calftail
Body: Dark green chenille
Wing: Grass green calftail, tied spent and
           angled slightly back
Head: Dark green chenille, tied to look
           like a continuation of the body

The Grubby Gert was introduced in the early 1970s by the Gaines Company of Pennsylvania as an addition to their Grubby Bug series of slow-sinking panfish flies. Gaines offers this fly in yellow, black and white as well as green.

HUM BUG

Hook: Straight eye, standard wire
Body: Yellow chenille
Legs: White rubber hackle
Back: Black chenille
Head: Black chenille

The Hum Bug is a fairly old panfish pattern and another in Gaines' Grubby Bug series. It was designed to fish just below the surface, and is be tied in many colors including yellow and brown, white and black, and red and white.

Tied by Tom Lentz

Tied by Tom Lentz

Tied by Jack Ellis

LOVE BUG

Hook: Standard dry, light wire
Body: Black closed cell foam body,
           segmented with thread
Hackle: Black
Head: Fluorescent orange

"Love bugs abound in Florida in May and again in September," writes Tom Lentz of Cocoa, Florida, and panfish feed on them with abandon. Love bugs mate in flight and often fall to the surface of the water coupled together; thus a double fly with a fore and aft hackle can be tied to imitate these mating insects.

MARABOU MISS

Hook: Down eye, standard wire
Tail: Fluorescent green marabou
Underbody: Lead wire
Body: White chenille
Wing: Fluorescent green marabou, with
             a couple of strands of pearlescent
             crystal flash on the side

The Marabou Miss is a popular wet fly that was developed by The Gaines Company as a part of their Grubby Bug series. Tom Lentz who ties this variation considers it his ". . . number one crappie fly." It is also effective on bluegills and the odd bass.

McDOUGAL, BUMBLE

Hook: Down eye, standard dry fly
Tail: Brown bucktail dyed yellow
Body: Bands of black and yellow dyed
           deer body hair, trimmed full
Wing: Cree or grizzly hackle tips
Hackle: Grizzly, cree, or variant dyed yel-
           low; or one yellow and one black
           hackle

Jack Ellis spends a lot of time pursuing panfish and trying to imitate the insects on which they feed. The Bumble McDougal is one of a series called the "Dixie McDougals" that was inspired by a well-known trout fly called the Rat-Face McDougal.

Panfish Flies

Tied by Jack Ellis

Tied by Farrow Allen

Tied by Farrow Allen

McDOUGAL, WASP

Hook: Down eye, 1X or 2X long, stan-
         dard wire
Tail: Bucktail or gray squirrel tail dyed
         orange
Body: Dyed brown deer body hair
Wing: Slender black hackle tips, long
Hackle: Cree, domestic variant, or grizzly
         dyed orange

Jack Ellis's Wasp is a part of his Dixie
McDougal series. Ellis reminds us that these
flies should be fished with a "jiggling movement to imitate a struggling insect."

McGINTY

Hook: Down eye, standard wire
Tail: Red hackle barbs over which is
         barred teal
Body: Yellow and black chenille
Hackle: Brown
Wing: White tipped mallard wing quill
         segment

A basic Bumble Bee imitation that bluegills
and crappie find irresistible throughout most
of the summer. It can also be tied as a dry fly
with an upright, divided wing and fished
very successfully on the surface.

MIDGE PUPA

Hook: Standard dry, light wire
Tail: Fine peacock herl from the eye
Abdomen: Stripped peacock quill or mixed
          dark and light moose mane
Thorax: Dark seal fur or similar with a few
          hairs picked out to imitate legs
Note: Colors may vary to match the
          natural insect.

Before hatching, midge pupa migrate in
large numbers from the bottom muck and
debris of lakes and rivers to hang vertically in
the surface film. As they drift in the surface
they are vulnerable to cruising panfish.

Tied by Dick Stewart

Tied by Tom Lentz

Tied by Farrow Allen

MINI MYLAR BRIM FLY

Hook: Down eye, 2X long, standard wire
Tail: Gray marabou
Body: Pearlescent Mylar tubing with the
         core removed, slipped over the
         hook and secured front and back
Note: Mylar tubing of any color may be
         combined with marabou of any
         color to arrive at whatever you
         imagine will please the bream.

Tom Lentz says "this is a good pattern when
brim or specks are feeding on small baitfish."
His favorite variation is tied with a fluorescent green tail and pearlescent Mylar tubing
over fluorescent green floss.

PANFISH POLECAT

Hook: Down eye, standard wire
Tail: Yellow marabou
Underbody: Lead wire
Legs: White rubber hackle, 4 legs on
           each side
Body: Black chenille, with a strip of yel-
           low chenille pulled forward, un-
           derneath

Jerry Riggens, of the Florida Flyrod Club,
tied the Polecat for brim fishing. Tom Lentz,
who tied this example, rates this fly "third in
what I consider the big-three brim flies."

PICKET PIN

Hook: Down eye, 2X or 3X long
Tail: Brown hackle barbs
Body: Peacock herl
Hackle: Brown, palmered over the body
Wing: Gray squirrel tail
Head: Peacock herl

The Picket Pin is one of the most versatile
panfish flies around. It can be fished as a wet
fly, a nymph, a streamer or even as a dry if
treated with flotant. The only drawback
may be the fragile nature of the peacock herl,
which can be reinforced with fine gold wire,
counter-wrapped through the head and body.

Tied by Dick Stewart

RENEGADE

Hook: Standard dry, light wire
Tag: Flat gold tinsel
Rear hackle: Brown
Body: Peacock herl
Front hackle: White

The Renegade was originated for trout fishing and has become extremely popular in the Rocky Mountain area. It is also popular for panfish and can be fished either dry or wet.

Tied by Jim Stewart

ROYAL BRIM KILLER

Hook: Down eye, heavy wire
Tail: A heavy loop of red wool yarn
Body: Black chenille, red floss and black chenille
Wing: Gray squirrel tail, long
Legs: White rubber hackle, long

Jim Stewart's Royal Brim Killer is so named because of the similarity to the body of the well-known Royal Coachman. Southern bluegills are very partial to red and this pattern of Stewart's, with its long rubber legs, is a killer.

Tied by Farrow Allen

SCUD (OLIVE)

Hook: Down eye, 1X long, humped
Tail: Olive hen hackle barbs
Body: Olive and black seal fur or substitute blended with dark hare's ear
Shellback: Clear plastic
Rib: Gold wire
Legs: Picked-out fur
Note: Also tied gray or brown, in hook sizes 8 to 12.

Scuds are commonly (although erroneously) called "fresh-water shrimp," and they inhabit many warmwater ponds.

Tied by Jim Stewart

STEWART'S HORNET

Hook: Down eye, heavy wire
Body: Brown and fluorescent yellow chenille
Legs: Yellow rubber hackle
Collar: Soft dark furnace or black hackle
Head: Fluorescent yellow

Jim Stewart tied this bluegill fly with standard yellow chenille in 1954 for Whiteville Lake in Tennessee. Today, nearly four decades later, using fluorescent chenille, the Hornet is still driving bluegills nuts.

Tied by Jack Ellis

WALNUT CATERPILLAR

Hook: Down eye, 4X long, slightly bent
Tail: Black goose biots
Butt: Black chenille
Body: Black chenille with an overbody and an underbody of yellow chenille pulled forward
Rib: Black hackle, clipped short
Head: Red chenille

Jack Ellis tied this fly to imitate a large black-and-yellow caterpillar that feeds on the foliage of pond and streamside hardwood trees. Regarding caterpillars in general, Ellis writes that because of "geographical diversity, each angler must observe . . . phenomena on his own home water."

Tied by Farrow Allen

WHITE TAIL PALMER GNAT

Hook: 3X or 4X long
Underbody: Lead wire (optional)
Tail: White rubber hackle
Body: Black chenille or wool, dressed slimly
Hackle: Black, tied in by the tip and palmered forward
Eyes: Silver bead chain eyes

Tom Nixon introduced this fly for bluegills ". . . quite some years back on the Current River, up from Cedar Grove, Missouri." The success of this fly, from Missouri to the tidal creeks of southwestern Louisiana, makes it a worthwhile addition to your fly box.

Poppers

Tied by The Gaines Company

BEE BUG

Hook:	Kinked shank popper hook		bumble bee
Body:	A slender tapered cork cylinder,	Wings:	Broad yellow-dyed or natural griz-
	rounded in the rear with a flat		zly hackle tips tied directly to the
	unslanted face. The Bee Bug is		cork body, two hackles per side
	usually painted yellow and black	Legs:	Rubber hackle tied on to the body
	or white and black to resemble a		along with the wings

This uniquely constructed bug comes from Tom Eggler of The Gaines Company, in Gaines, Pennsylvania, where it has been in continuous production since the the 1950s. It's a popular pattern for bass in large sizes and for bluegill and crappie in small sizes.

Tied by Sheldon Bolstad

BOLSTAD FOAM DIVER

Hook:	Straight eye, standard wire	Body:	Yellow floating foam, trimmed
Tail:	Yellow calftail or bucktail over		into a wedge-shape diving head,
	which is pearlescent yellow crystal		slit on the bottom and cemented
	flash		to the hook as shown
Skirt:	Red hackle	Eyes:	Hollow plastic

The current president of The Smallmouth Alliance, Sheldon Bolstad of Minneapolis, developed the Foam Diver as part of a series of foam-body bugs. Bolstad ties his foam flies in many shapes and says all of them are easy to make, that they cast better than deer-hair bugs and will float forever.

Tied by Frank Theobald

FOAM SANDAL BUG

Hook:	Kinked shank popper hook	Body:	Foam cylinder cut from the lami-
Tail:	Several pairs of broad webby griz-		nated sole of a beach sandal
	zly hackles tied flat and curving	Legs:	Three pairs of rubber hackle
	down		threaded through the body with a
Skirt:	Grizzly hackle		needle and pliers

Frank Theobald, of The Fly Fishing Shop in Glenside, Pennsylvania, has perfected the procedure of converting discarded recreational footwear into colorful, rugged popping bugs. The multi-color laminated soles of beach sandals are easily cut and sanded into a variety of useful shapes.

Tied by Lefty Kreh

LEFTY'S BUG

Hook:	Kinked shank popper hook	Note:	It is very important that the hook
Tail:	Red or gray squirrel tail		be as close to the flat bottom of the
Body:	Tapered cork or balsa wood cylin-		body as possible. This enables the
	der, cut flat on the bottom with a		popper to hang in the water with
	flat face, angled back and painted		the tail down, which is critical to
	bright yellow or fluorescent or-		the appearance and the hooking
	ange with prominent eyes		properties of Lefty's Bug.

Lefty Kreh developed this bug many years ago while guiding for smallmouth on the Potomac, Susquehanna and Shenandoah Rivers. It is a simple pattern that Kreh says casts better and picks up easier than its heavy-hackled, rubber-legged companions. Bugs with a flat, slanted face are sometimes referred to as skipping bugs.

MINNOW

Hook:	Kinked shank popper hook		cupped face, painted as desired
Tail:	Two pairs of webby hackles, curving out	Legs:	Rubber hackle, threaded through the body with a needle and pliers, two facing forward and two backward
Skirt:	Several wraps of hackle		
Body:	A short cork body with sharply tapered back and a slanted, deeply		

The Minnow is an early popping bug that dates back to the 1930s and was first sold commercially by the E. H. Peckinpaugh Company of Chattanooga, Tennessee. Before becoming a successful fly manufacturer, Ernest Peckinpaugh was a Chattanooga building contractor who spent most of his spare time chasing bass and panfish or tying flies for his friends.

Tied by The Gaines Company

NINNY BUG

Hook:	Kinked shank popper hook		bottom, painted as desired
Tail:	Short tuft of floss over longer rubber hackles	Legs:	Rubber hackle threaded through the body with a needle and pliers, two pairs facing forward and two backward
Skirt:	Several wraps of hackle		
Body:	A round cork body with a flat		

The Ninny Bug is a slider with a gently rounded shape that is designed to create a subtle, quiet wake as opposed to a loud pop or gurgle. It's especially fished for panfish in the Gulf Coast states where this style of bug has been popularized by Tony Accardo's popper company in Baton Rouge, Louisiana.

Tied by The Gaines Company

OLD JOE

Hook:	Kinked shank popper hook		slightly slanted flat face, painted as desired
Tail:	One or two pairs of webby hackle, curving out	Legs:	Rubber hackle, threaded through the body with a needle and pliers, two facing forward and two facing backward
Skirt:	Several wraps of hackle, usually the same color as the tail		
Body:	Tapered cork cylinder with a		

In Tom Eggler's booklet, *Fishing Popping Bugs for Bass and Panfish,* he describes the Old Joe with its flat slanted face as a "skipping bug." This versatile shape lets the angler skip and dance the bug on the surface or slide it quietly through vegetation.

Tied by The Gaines Company

PAN POP

Hook:	Kinked shank popper hook		well as fly-tying shops. The shape is unmodified but used as is and painted as desired
Tail:	A pair of webby hackles, curving out		
Skirt:	Several wraps of hackle	Legs:	Rubber hackle, threaded through the center of the body with a needle and pliers
Body:	A basic "bottle stopper" shaped cork body available in hardware as		

Tom Eggler describes the Pan Pop as "... the easiest and most basic bug ... because the body requires no cutting or shaping." The Pan Pop's flat, unslanted face makes for a versatile bug that you can skip, slide or pop. Turn the cork around and you'll have a "Stopper Popper," a bug that doesn't create a lot of surface commotion and fishes well in clear or shallow water over shy fish.

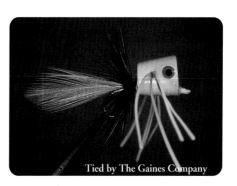
Tied by The Gaines Company

Poppers

Tied by Edge Water Fishing Products

PENCIL POPPER

Hook:	Long shank, straight eye	Body:	Closed cell foam pencil shape popper
Tail:	Dark over light marabou with a few strands of pearl Flashabou on top	Eyes:	Solid plastic

The long, slender shape of the Pencil Popper is naturally suited for imitating a wounded minnow struggling on the surface. The narrowness also provides an extremely aerodynamic shape that makes pencil-shaped poppers easier to cast than bulkier designs.

Tied by Thornapple Orvis Shop

POBST FROG

Hook:	Keel fly	Skirt:	Yellow hackle
Body:	Slotted cork body, painted frog-like and mounted onto the hook as shown	Note:	After the fly is completed, bend the hook point up until it is parallel to the top of the top of the cork body. This will provide better hooking.
Legs:	Green deer body hair, divided and cocked up slightly		

Developed by Dick Pobst of the Thornapple Orvis Shop in Ada, Michigan, who was the original designer of the Keel Hook, a design which enabled the construction of many weedless flies.

Tied by Dick Stewart

ROCKER POPPER

Hook:	Straight eye, long shank		choice
Weight:	Several wraps of lead wire made at the bend of the hook	Body:	Round cork or foam, painted the color of your choice
Tail and skirt: Rubber hackle, color of your			

We first saw this design some ten years age and believe the concept originated somewhere in the south-central states. With the Rocker Popper you can cast to very small openings among the lilies, and then work the fly within this limited space. Short, one or two inch tugs on your fly line cause the fly to rock and dip, making the rubber hackle sway and breathe, and the weight returns the fly to its upright position.

Tied by The Gaines Company

SNEAKY PETE

Hook:	Kinked shank popper hook		down to a pointed nose at the eye of the hook
Tail:	Rubber hackle over which is a short tuft of floss	Legs:	Rubber hackle, threaded through the body with a needle and pliers, two facing forward and two backward
Skirt:	Several wraps of hackle		
Body:	"Reverse tapered" cork cylinder, with a flat slanted back, tapering		

The Sneaky Pete is an old Gaines "sliding" bug that Tom Eggler says is one of the best known and most widely used cork-bodied flies around. Sliders are often used on bright days for fishing in clear water when bass and panfish are more likely to be spooked than attracted by the loud disturbance of a popping bug.

SELECT BIBLIOGRAPHY

BOOKS

Bergman, Ray.1932. *Just fishing*. Philadelphia: The Penn Publishing Company.
_____.1947. *With fly, plug, and bait*. New York: William Morrow & Company.
Boyle, Robert H. and Dave Whitlock, ed. 1975. *Fly-tyer's almanac*. New York: Crown Publishers, Inc.
_____.1978. *Second fly-tyer's almanac*. Philadelphia & New York: J.B. Lippincott.
Brooks, Joe. 1947. *Bass bug fishing*. New York: A.S. Barnes and Company.
Eggler, Tom. 1987. *Fishing popping bugs for bass & panfish*. Gaines, PA: The Gaines Company.
Henshall, James A. [1881] 1970, 1978. *Book of the black bass*. Montgomery, Alabama: Bass Anglers
                  Sportsman Society of America, Inc.
Leiser, Eric. 1987. *The book of fly patterns*. New York: Alfred A. Knopf.
Livingston, A.D. 1977. *Tying bugs and flies for bass*. Philadelphia & New York: J.B. Lippincott.
Murray, Harry. 1989. *Fly fishing for smallmouth bass*. New York: Lyons & Burford.
Nixon, Tom. [1968] 1977. *Fly tying and fly fishing for bass and panfish*. 2d ed., rev. South
                  Brunswick & New York: A.S. Barnes and Company, Inc.
Stewart, Dick. 1989. *Bass Flies*. Intervale, NH: Northland Press.
_____& Bob Leeman. 1982. *Trolling flies for trout and salmon*. Brattleboro, VT: Stephen Greene
                  Press.
Sturgis, William Bayard. 1940. *Fly-tying*. New York: Charles Scribner's Sons.
Whitlock, Dave. 1982. *Dave Whitlock's guide to aquatic trout foods*. New York: Lyons & Burford.

PERIODICALS

American Angler. various dates 1990 - 1992. Intervale, NH: Northland Press.
American Angler & Fly Tyer. various dates 1988 - 1990. Intervale, NH: Northland Press.
American Fly Tyer. various dates 1986 - 1987. Intervale, NH: Northland Press.

INDEX TO FLY DRESSINGS

A
Adams — 60
Albino Serpent — 22
Angus (Black) — 30

B
Baby Seal — 72
Badger Streamer — 30
Bandy-Legged Muddler — 30
Bass Buddy — 31
Bass Bugger (Purple and Pink) — 31
BBX — 72
'Becca's Bug — 2
Bee Bug — 78
Betts' Bull-it-Head (Bass Fry) — 31
Betts' Bull-it Head (Flashdancer) — 2
Betts' Bull-it Head (Frog) — 2
Betts' Foam Dragonfly — 60
Big Ugly — 66
Bitch Creek — 66
Bivisible (Brown) — 72
Black Ghost Marabou — 32
Black Nose Dace — 32
Bolstad Foam Diver — 78
Bolstad Skipping Minnow — 32
Bolstad Sputter Minnow — 33
Brass Hare — 29
Brass Wonder (Olive) — 72
Brass Wonder (Silver) — 72
Brim Bug Eye — 72
Brim Fly (Gray) — 73
Brim Special — 73
Bristleback — 33
Brown's Crayfish — 18
Bucktail Muddler (Natural) — 33
Bug Eye Integration — 34
Bullet Bug — 26
Bumble Bee — 73

C
Cajun Coachman — 73
Calcasieu Pig Boat — 34
Cardinelle — 34
Casual Dress — 66
Catalpa Worm — 73
Caterpillar — 73
Chantière — 26
Chenille Bug (Gray) — 74
Clay's Crayfish — 18
Clouser Crayfish — 18
Clouser Crippled Minnow — 35
Clouser Deep Minnow (Perch) — 35
Clouser Deep Minnow (Ultra) — 35
Clouser Hellgrammite — 66
Clouser Sil-E Frog — 12
Clouser Swimming Nymph — 67
Cooper Bug see Devil Bug
Crawdad Shedder — 18
Crazy-Legs Spider — 3
Creature — 10
Crippled Perch — 36
Curl-Tail Leech — 20

D
Dahlberg Dilg-Slider — 3
Dahlberg Diver (Original) — 26
Dahlberg Flashdancer — 36
Dahlberg Floating Minnow — 36
Dahlberg Frog Diver — 12
Dahlberg Fur Strip Diver — 27
Dahlberg Horse Popper — 3
Dahlberg Mega-Diver — 27
Dahlberg Mega-Slop Slider — 4
Dahlberg Skipper Frog — 12
Dave's Frog Diver — 13
Dave's Hopper — 60
Debbie's Sunny — 37
Deep Black — 74
Deer-Hair Mouse — 10
Devil Bug (Red) — 74
Dick's Down East Smelt — 37
Dixie McDougal see McDougal, Bumble
Doodle Bug see Devil Bug
Doug's Hair Moth — 60
Dragon Fly Nymph — 67
Dragonfly Nymph Muddler — 67
Drake's Slider see Wounded Minnow
Dredgebug (Brown) — 67

E
Eel — 22
Elk Hair Caddis (Brown) — 61
Egg Sucking Jig Leech — 29
E.S. Minnow (Shad) — 37

F
Farmer's Field Mouse — 10
Farmer's Silicone Frog — 13
Fathead Diver — 74
Featherwing Moth — 61
Flat Bug — 4
Foam Beetle — 61
Foam Caterpillar — 61
Foam Dragonfly — 62
Foamin' Bass Bugs Foamin' Perch — 38
Foam Sandal Bug — 78
Fur Leech — 20
Fuzzabou Shad — 38

G
Gerbubble Bug see Whitlock's Gerbubble Bug
Gill Bugger — 74
Gill Getter — 74
Gill Slider — 75
Girdle Bug — 68
Goddard Caddis — 62
Gold-ribbed Hare's Ear Nymph see Hare's Ear Nymph
Gray Ghost — 38
Green Darner Nymph — 68
Grubby Gert — 75

H
Hard-Bodied Ant (Black) — 62
Hare's Ear Nymph — 68
Hellgrammite — 68

Henshall Bug — 4
Holschlag Hackle Fly — 29
Hornberg Special — 39
Hornberg Streamer — 39
Hum Bug — 75

I
Improved Sofa Pillow — 62

J
Jimminy Cricket — 63
Joe's Hopper — 63
Jonathan — 5
June Bug — 5

K
Katie's Pet — 11
Keel Bug (Yellow/Black) — 39

L
Larry's Leech — 20
Lead Eyed Bunny Booger — 40
Lefty's Bug — 78
Lefty's Red & White — 40
Letort Cricket — 63
Letort Hopper — 63
Li'l Pickerel — 40
Llama — 41
Lopez Minnow — 41
Louisiana Mickey Finn — 41
Love Bug — 75

M
Marabou Miss — 75
Marabou Muddler (White) — 42
Marabou Streamer (Yellow) — 42
Matuka (Olive) — 42
McDougal, Bumble — 75
McDougal, Wasp — 76
McEelworm — 22
McGinty — 76
McNally Magnum — 43
McSnake — 23
Melody Mouse — 11
Messinger Bucktail Diver Frog — 14
Messinger Bucktail Frog — 13
Messinger Bucktail Popper Frog — 14
Messinger Leap Frog — 14
Michigan Hopper see Joe's Hopper
Mickey Finn — 43
Midge Pupa — 76
Mini Mylar Brim Fly — 76
Minnow — 79
Miracle Minnow see Miracle Perch
Miracle Perch — 43
Mississippi Bass Bug see Ozark Weedless Bucktail
Miss Westwood's Bass Bug see Ozark Weedless Bucktail
Mizzolian (Missoulian) Spook — 44
Montana — 69
Mosquito — 64
Muddler Hopper see Dave's Hopper
Muddler Minnow — 44

Murray's Hellgrammite 69
Murray's Strymph 69

N Neptune Streamer 44
Ninny Bug 79
Nitehummer 64

O Old Joe 79
Oscar's Hexagenia Nymph 69
Ozark Weedless Bucktail 45

P Panfish Polecat 76
Pan Pop 79
Pencil Popper 80
Perkiomen Muddler 5
Pic-A-Bugger 45
Picket Pin 76
Pobst Frog 80
Polyfrog 15
Polywog 15
Pop Lips Crayfish 19
Pop Lips Frog 15
Pop Lips Perch 45
Pop Lips Pumpkinseed 46
Pop Lips Shiner 46
Powder Puff 6

R Rat-Face McDougal see
              McDougal, Bumble
Rattlin' Bluegill 46
Red & White Bucktail 47
Renegade 77
Richelieu 6
River Witch 70
Rocker Popper 80
Robinson's Mud Bug 19
Royal Brim Killer 77

S Sang Frog 16
Sang Sinking Frog 16
Scud (Olive) 77
Shenk's Sculpin (Black) 47
Shenk's White Streamer 47
Shineabou Shad 48
Shineabou Shad (Wool Head) 48
Shineabou Shiner 48
Shineabou Shiner (Wool Head) 49
Shineabou Sunfish 49
Shineabou Sunfish (Wool Head) 49
Silver Doctor see
         Waterman's Silver Outcast
Sneaky Pete 80
Sowela 50
Spuddler 50
Stewart's Bass-A-Roo 27
Stewart's Buzz Bug (Purple Back) 6
Stewart's Chub Darter (Blue/Black) 50
Stewart's Dancing Frog 16
Stewart's Dying Sidewinder Shiner 51

Stewart's Fuzzy Wuzzy 23
Stewart's Hair Spoon Frog 17
Stewart's Hornet 77
Stewart's Jointed Popper 7
Stewart's Lucky Wiggler 28
Stewart's Rattle Worm 23
Stewart's Spin-In-Jim 7
Stopper Popper see Pan Pop
Swimming Crayfish 19

T Tap's Deer Hair 7
Ted's Stonefly 70
Tête de Boule (Orange) 51
Thief 51
Thom Green Leech 21
Thunder Creek see Polyfrog
Tippet Whisker 52
Tom's Bandit 52
Troth Bullhead 52
Ty's Tantalizer (Improved) 28

U Ugly Bug 20

W Walnut Caterpillar 77
Water Moccasin 24
Waterman's Silver Outcast 53
Weedless Wooly (Yellow) 53
Whistler (Red & White) 53
White Hair Moth 64
White Tail Grizzly 54
White Tail Palmer Gnat 77
Whitlock's Bass Hopper 64
Whitlock's Chamois Leech 21
Whitlock's Chamois Lizard 24
Whitlock's Damsel 65
Whitlock's Damsel Nymph (Brown) 70
Whitlock's Deep Sheep Crappie 54
Whitlock's Dragon Nymph (Olive) 70
Whitlock's Eelworm Streamer 24
Whitlock's Floating Muddler 8
Whitlock's Gerbubble Bug 8
Whitlock's Hare Diver 28
Whitlock's Hare Grub 54
Whitlock's Hare Jig Fly 29
Whitlock's Hare Waterpup 25
Whitlock's Hare Worm 25
Whitlock's Hellgrammite 71
Whitlock's 'Lectric Leech 21
Whitlock's Match-the-Minnow
                          (Perch) 55
Whitlock's Matuka Sculpin (Tan) 55
Whitlock's Most Whit Hair Bug 8
Whitlock's Mouserat 11
Whitlock's Multicolor Muddler 55
Whitlock's Near Nuff Frog 17
Whitlock's Red Squirrel Nymph 71
Whitlock's Prismatic Shiner 56
Whitlock's Sheep Shad 56
Whitlock's Sheep Sunfish 56

Whitlock's Softshell Crayfish 19
Whitlock's Spent Krystal Dragon 65
Whitlock's Water Snake Diver 25
Whitlock's Wigglelegs Frog 17
Wiggle Bug (Purple) 9
Wiggle Tail 57
Wilder Dilg Feather Minnow see
               Dahlberg Dilg-Slider
Wilder-Dilg Slider see
               Dahlberg Dilg-Slider
Wilkie's Beauty (Yellow) 9
Wilkie's Runt 57
Wilkie's Shad 57
Wobbling-Wounded Bluegill 58
Woolfolk Minnow 58
Woolly Bugger 58
Woolly Bugger (Crystal Chenille) 59
Wooly Worm (Yellow) 71
Wounded Minnow 59
Wulff, Gray 65
Wulff, White 65

Y Yellow-Crowned Night Heron 9
Yuk Bug 71

Z Zonker (Pearl & Gray) 59

ABOUT THE AUTHORS

Dick Stewart (left) and Farrow Allen

Dick Stewart, has been tying bass flies since the age of fourteen and has been professionally involved in the fly-fishing industry for almost twenty years. He has authored or co-authored five books including the fly-tying primer *Bass Flies* and the best-selling *Universal Fly Tying Guide*. His bass fishing experience began in Pennsylvania and includes fly fishing in New England and eastern Canada. Dick has settled in the White Mountains area of New Hampshire where he is Publisher of *American Angler* magazine.

Farrow Allen, moved from New York City to Vermont where for twelve years he owned a fly-fishing shop in the Burlington area. During this time he co-authored a book *Vermont Trout Streams*. A long time fly tier, Farrow has fished for bass in central Canada and throughout the northeast, especially in the Adirondacks of New York. Currently he is associated with *American Angler* magazine and resides in New Hampshire.

ABOUT THIS BOOK

This is the third book in a series of five which cover the majority of recognized fly patterns in use in the United States and Canada. The series is entitled *Fishing Flies of North America* and the individual titles are as follows:

Flies for Atlantic Salmon
Flies for Steelhead
Flies for Bass & Panfish
Flies for Saltwater
Flies for Trout